HOW TO ROCK SELF-PUBLISHING

A Rage Against the Manuscript guide

STEFF GREEN

ISBN: 978-0-9951342-7-0

❀ Created with Vellum

HOW TO ROCK SELF-PUBLISHING

- Do you have a story you're bursting to tell the world?
- Are you sick of being rejected by the publishing establishment?
- Do you want to inject a little punk rock, DIY ethos into your indie author career?

In *How to Rock Self-Publishing*, bestselling indie author and publishing coach Steff Green shows you how to tell your story, find your readers, and build a badass author brand.

As a self-published author you'll learn how to:

- Define your measure of success and set attainable goals.
- Create an exciting author brand you want to write under forever.
- Tame your monkey mind and consolidate your gazillion ideas into a solid plan.
- Choose the best platforms, editors, designers, and tools to create a high-quality book.

- Plan a compelling book series in any genre that will have your readers chomping for more.
- Write faster, release more often, and enjoy what you create.
- Spot trends and gaps in the market where you can add your unique voice.
- Publish your book in print, ebook, and audio with all the nuts and bolts.
- Launch with a BANG! – including handy launch checklists.
- Create an engaging author platform to turn your readers into lifelong fans.
- Find unique and emerging opportunities in self-publishing to build your audience and earn a living.

Steff breaks down the 11-step process that's seen her go from failed archaeologist and obscure music blogger to a *USA Today* bestseller with a six-figure income. With dozens of examples from across the publishing landscape and real-talk from her own career, Steff shows how imagination, creativity, and perseverance can help you achieve your dreams.

How to Rock Self-Publishing isn't just a book about writing, it's about grabbing your dreams by the balls, living faster, harder and louder, and cranking your art up to 11.

Chapter One

SO YOU'RE READY TO START SELF-PUBLISHING

You've been working hard to hone your writing chops and create work you're proud of, and now you're ready to share it with the world.

Perhaps you've approached a publisher already and been pushed back, or maybe you have a small audience online and you want to know how to deliver something meatier than a blog post. Maybe you're a writer with the dream of seeing your name on the spine of a real book, or perhaps you're excited about the possibilities of making writing your full-time career. Maybe you're all of those things. Or none of them.

Whatever kind of writer you are, allow me to welcome you to the wild, crazy, frustrating, and wonderful world of self-publishing.

Digital reading and self-publishing through platforms like Amazon KDP, Apple Books, and Kobo Writing Life have opened up tremendous opportunities for writers to get their work directly in the hands of their readers. We no longer need a publisher to make a book and get it found. This means we can keep the majority of our royalties instead of sharing them with a big corporation. Because of this, writers all over the world can find their voice and audience, make a profit, and write full-time. It sounds awesome, and it is.

But...

...there's a steep learning curve from being a penmonkey hiding in your cat pile to become your own publisher. You're no longer just a writer – you have to be the editor, designer, business manager, marketing department, *and* tea-and-sandwiches person.

What's fantastic about this route is that there are many paths to success – every day I'm amazed by stories of writers making it big and finding their readers in new and unique ways. This book is mainly about my own experience and the things I've learned so far, but I've tried to also include lots of stories about other writers I'm lucky enough to know to show you that you don't have to do things 'my way' to succeed.

I've set out *How to Rock Self-Publishing* as a set of eleven... let's call them guidelines. I don't like to call anything a 'rule,' because for every 'rule' I believe exists, I can point to a writer who is killing it breaking that rule. But they are *guidelines* that can help steer you to a path of least resistance and put you in the best possible position to hit your writing and publishing goals. If your ultimate dream is to quit your day job to write full time, then paying attention to these guidelines will help you get there.

This book is short, but it's absolutely packed with information. It's going to feel a little overwhelming – but I hope it will also inspire you to action. What I want to do is show you all the possibilities that are open with self-publishing, and leave it up to you to choose the path that suits you best. Don't feel as though you have to do everything – but you should definitely start with something.

The main thing I want you to take away from this guide is just how possible it is to be a successful self-published author, that there are many different paths to success, and give you some solid next steps for your particular project. Are you ready? Let's get writing!

Chapter Two
WHO AM I?

Just so you know that I'm not talking out my arse, I'll tell you a little about my writing career and success with self-publishing.

I'm Steff. I'm a New Zealander. I love to brew my own mead and cuddle my cats, and I'm legally blind. I grew up in a small town with book characters as my only friends. I was a genuinely weird kid who sucked at sports and had an unhealthy obsession with Ancient Egypt... incidentally, I grew up into a weird adult who still sucks at sports and I still have an unhealthy obsession with Ancient Egypt. Reading was an escape for me, and from a very young age I wrote stories about worlds I invented and the people who inhabited them.

I wrote all through high school and university, finishing around four full-length novels that are all completely terrible. I sent one off to a publisher's mailing address I got from the back of a Baby-Sitters Club book and received a very encouraging form rejection.

Fast-forward a few years. I went to university to study archaeology. I got a postgraduate degree and volunteered in every museum and for every excavation that came up. When I finished my studies, I tried to find a job, but after a year of searching, no one would hire me. I was told I was a 'health and safety' risk because of my wonky eyes. After a museum curator said I "couldn't be trusted" around artifacts, I took the bus home in tears.

After about eight months of these kinds of rejections, my husband couldn't bear to see me continue to put myself through this farce of trying to prove I *could* work. He suggested I consider a different career path. "If you look at it this way, you've done archaeology. You've been on all these digs and achieved all these cool things other people don't normally get to do. Maybe you could think about what you'd like to do after that – and it should be something where no one can say, 'You can't do this.'"

As soon as he said that, my mind went to those half-finished novels saved on my hard drive. I always wanted to be a writer. It was something I could do by myself, without someone hovering over me waiting for me to fail.

But I didn't know how to become a writer. I had no idea how writers earned money or what I should do next. Did I have to go back to university? Who hired writers? Did I possess the requisite number of cats?

I did what any self-respecting Millennial would do. I Googled 'how to make a living from your writing' and proceeded to try everything on the list.

I pitched articles to magazines. I started a blog. I wrote product descriptions for gothic corsets and glittery wall paint. I got my first cheque for $10.50 for an article I wrote. Then another for $25, for $55, for $180. I kept pitching magazines, offering my services to businesses, and selling myself. I learned that I couldn't take rejection personally because then I could never move forward.

I never gave up.

Most importantly, I pulled out an old novel and finished it. I pitched it to an editor at a writer's conference, and she asked to read it. I felt as though I could taste my dream. Just one final hurdle, one more gatekeeper, and I'd be there!

But the publishing world moves slowly, and interest is not the same as a book deal. After working with that editor on three different manuscripts over five or so years, I got the call every writer dreams about. I had a publishing deal! Three science fiction books over four years. I couldn't believe it. I'd made it!

Then my editor retired, and the publisher decided to cut her list in half. My book went on the chopping block, and it didn't survive. I was devastated. So many years of work and I'd have to start all over again. Yet again, someone had told me, 'You can't do this.'

Around that time, writers like Hugh Howey and Amanda Hocking were talking about how well they were doing self-publishing ebooks on Amazon. I decided to take one of my trunked novels and self-publish that to see if I liked the experience. It was a terrible book that sold exactly 122 copies, but I loved editing it and designing a cover and promoting it. I loved that no one told me I couldn't do it.

I was hooked.

Next, I started to self-publish the Engine Ward series of weird science fiction books, in both paperback and Kindle editions. They sold okay – 10-20 copies a month or so, but I didn't feel like I was any closer to my dream of being a full-time writer.

One day, I attended a party where a friend and I were discussing *50 Shades of Grey*. This friend loved the books, and I'd read the first chapter and couldn't continue because of the writing style and grammar (or lack thereof).

I was bitching about this book's success when my friend

cut in to say, "It's not as if you could write a sexy book like that, Steff."

I nodded in agreement and changed the subject, because she was right. I wasn't being supportive of another woman's success or about my friend's tastes. Also, in my group of sexually adventurous friends, I'm known for being quite private about my sex life and, well, I can't say the word 'penis' without blushing. Of *course* I couldn't write a book like that.

Of course not.

I mean, c'mon.

But in my head, the cogs were turning.

Challenge accepted.

In secret, without telling anyone, I wrote a 30,000-word story about a fox shapeshifter named Ryan who lived as a reclusive artist, and the gallery curator who brought him out of his shell. There's a shifter war and an unhinged brother and a crumbling medieval manor and all sorts of murder and chaos and intrigue. I'd never had so much fun or found the words came so easily.

I paid $50 for a cover and published *Art of Cunning* in April 2015 under a secret pen name – Steffanie Holmes. I expected nothing to happen except that one day when I wasn't so mortified about the sex in it I could show it to my friend and we'd both have a laugh.

I sold 1,000 copies in the first week.

I couldn't believe it. I kept expecting Amazon to call me up and say they'd given me someone else's royalties by mistake. But they never called, and the sales kept coming. I had to sheepishly tell my husband that I'd made all this money from my books, but it wasn't from my super-serious science fiction but a smutty fox shifter romance story.

After he got done laughing, he said, "Are you going to write more?"

(Spoiler alert: I wrote more).

Fast-forward to now. I've published over 35 books in total, most of them paranormal romance novels as Steffanie Holmes. I quit my day job in Feb 2018 to live the dream life of a full-time writer. I earn six-figures a year from my writing and have the most incredible fun doing it.

I am so insanely lucky and grateful, and that's why I've written this guide – because I want you to be able to share in the joy of telling stories of the heart and seeing your writing find an audience.

MY SELF-PUBLISHED BOOKS

The same week I left my day job, I released my first reverse harem novel, *The Castle of Earth and Embers*, book 1 of the Briarwood Witches series. Reverse harem, in case you don't know, is a romance trope where the heroine falls in love with not one but three-or-more heroes who all love her back. In the end, instead of choosing one of them, she has a happily-ever-after with all of them. Reverse harem became a trend in 2017, with many books hitting the Amazon bestseller lists around the time I wrote this book.

Up until this point, I'd been doing well off the back of my previous paranormal romance novels, but it's thanks to the Briarwood Witches series that my career took off. It felt like a sign from the universe that I'd made the right decision.

Before the release of *The Castle of Earth and Embers*, I was earning between $2,000-4,000 per month on Amazon, and about $1,000-2,000 on the other stores. Since I started releasing the Briarwood Witches books, my income climbed to $4k, $6k, $10k, and up.

I released 5 books in that series throughout 2018, approximately 1 book every 2 months. Each novel was around 80-100k in length. In December 2018, I released the box set of the complete series.

In January of 2019, I released *A Dead and Stormy Night*, book one in another reverse harem series – the Nevermore Bookshop Mysteries. What's been interesting about this series is that it doesn't follow the typical conventions of a romance book. I planned it based around a cozy mystery plot, but with reverse harem elements. It was a gamble, but that gamble paid off – the Nevermore Bookshop series has been even more successful so far than the Briarwood Witches, and it's so much fun to write.

In May of 2019, I noticed a lot of readers on Facebook groups asking for 'bully romance' books. I'd never heard the term before, so I read a couple and got completely hooked. I never planned to write one, but one day the idea for *Shunned* came to me in a dream. I dropped everything, wrote a blurb and made a placeholder cover, put a pre-order up on Amazon, and then wrote the book in 3 weeks. This book just poured out of me – it reminded me of the time I first tried writing romance. I felt like I was on to something magical.

I was right.

When *Shunned* released, it hit 45 in **the entire Amazon store**. It stayed in the top 100 for five days. In 30+ books, it's the first time I've ever had a real hit, and this series has changed my life. It's introduced my writing to tens of thousands of new readers and has enabled me to step up my career in a big way.

I'm telling you this because, throughout this book, I'll be referring to my own books. They are my most readily available sources for examples and learning. You might like to read them to see how I put the lessons in this book into practice to create a six-figure income self-publishing. I'll also refer to other books and authors, and to resources to help you along the way.

Getting to the point where I wrote my resignation letter took 3 years of serious work, 30 self-published books, and a stubborn refusal to be disheartened by my approximately 7 million mistakes. Now I'm publishing more than ever, doing amazing projects like launching a Kickstarter campaign for my first-ever children's book (https://www.kickstarter.com/projects/steffmetal/little-death-stands-up-to-bullies-in-a-gothic-pict), and speaking at events around the world. I'm working every day from my home library buried under a mountain of cats. I'm not going to lie – it's a very nice life.

I want you to have the success you dream of. I want you to be able to tell your stories and find the readers who need them. I want you to build a sustainable long-term writing career (if that's your dream) and give back my knowledge and enthusiasm to a community that has given me so so so much. That's why I wrote this book. I really hope you get something out of it, and out of the self-publishing experience. It's been one of the most rewarding things I've done in my life – may it be so for you.

Chapter Three

WHAT EVEN IS SELF-PUBLISHING?

Before we dive into the nitty-gritty details of how to do the thing, let's talk about what self-publishing is and what it isn't, as well as the history of self-pub. I promise the good stuff is coming, but I think it's worthwhile looking at the context of self-publishing before you dive in. It's like reviewing a new Iron Maiden album without ever listening to *The Number of the Beast*.

Self-publishing is an author bringing their book to market themselves, instead of going through a publishing house. The author is responsible not just for writing the book, but for making the cover, finding editors, formatting a manuscript, and finding a way to get it into the hands of readers. The author might do these things themselves or outsource them, but the key to self-publishing is that the author **retains control** over the process.

Self-publishing has been around for a long time. British satirist Laurence Sterne self-published the first two volumes of *Tristram Shandy*. Nathaniel Hawthorne, Emily Dickinson, Walt Whitman, and Jane Austen all experimented with self-publishing their work. Self-publishing of pamphlets and zines have been key to most underground movements throughout history, from occultists in the 17th and 18th centuries to political movements, activism, and the punk and heavy metal music scenes.

In the 20th century, self-publishing was mainly referred to by a derisive term, 'vanity press.' It used to be that if you were an author who'd exhausted the options for having your book traditionally published, you only really had a few options left. You could toss your manuscript under the bed and write something else, you could look for a small press, or you could pay a vanity press a large sum of money to print thousands of copies of your book, which you'd then have to hand-sell to readers.

Many of these self-publishing companies are little more than scam artists preying on the desires of authors to see their work in print. They often send 'acceptance' letters to potential authors, explaining their work has been 'selected' for publication and will be printed as soon as the invoice is paid. These authors had no understanding of how the publishing industry worked and assumed this was how all publishers operated. They'd happily fork over their $10,000 to have a box of books printed which they would then foist upon sympathetic friends and family.

Because of this, if you said 'self-publishing' to an industry professional, it would conjure up images of a well-meaning writer selling boxes of poorly-edited memoirs, poetry books, or religious treatises from the trunk of their car. Self-publishing was a dirty word, not discussed in polite company, and certainly not a threat to the status quo.

Very few of these vanity press books made it big on the mainstream. Those that did were usually non-fiction books from authors on the speaker circuit. They'd print a book to sell at the back of the room after their talks, and as their audience got bigger and their ideas spread, traditional publishers saw the potential for their work to reach a wider audience.

Two pieces of technology have transformed self-publishing in the last twenty years. The first is print-on-demand technology. This is where books are printed one at a time as they're ordered. I place an order on Amazon for a book. Amazon then prints one copy of that book and sends it out to me. The author doesn't have to set up a website or fulfillment system – they just collect a royalty.

POD books have enabled authors to sell print books with little to no overhead while removing the tricky fulfillment process. The downside is that POD lacks economy of scale, which means the books tend to be priced higher than traditionally published books that can be printed in bulk. This matters less than you might assume for reasons I'll get into next.

The second thing that changed self-publishing was the Kindle. Ebooks existed before the Kindle (which also wasn't the first ereader on the market), but they were usually sold as PDF documents to be read on a computer screen. This worked for some non-fiction publishers, but it was hard to convince readers to enjoy fiction on a screen. You couldn't curl up in front of the fire with a cup of tea, and since most websites were free, people didn't see why they should pay for digital content.

Some specialist publishers like Ellora's Cave (which sold erotic ebooks for women as downloadable files and thrived in the 90s and early 2000s) found success in the digital market. Ellora's Cave understood that women didn't want to read books with racy covers and titles in public, but they would do it on their lunch break or when their families were in bed. Most free erotic content on the internet was written by men for men and didn't give women what they were looking for. Ellora's Cave served a niche, and they made it their business to understand what their audience craved. We're going to be talking about niches throughout this book.

Despite Ellora's Cave leading by example, most publishers couldn't capture online readers with PDFs and expensive ebooks.

What the Kindle did when it launched in 2007 was give readers the ability to enjoy digital books in the same way they currently enjoyed their print books. It appealed to aging and print-disabled readers who liked the ability to enlarge print, and to travelers and commuters who wanted a portable library. It offered an e-ink screen that recreated the experience of print, without the eye-strain of a screen's glare.

Originally, only a few books were available to readers in the Kindle store. Many publishers thought it was a fad and didn't bother adding their books to the Kindle library. Amazon wanted to offer readers more options. They realized they'd never be able to sell Kindles if they couldn't offer anything for readers to actually *read*. They needed to fill their library with more content, and when they couldn't get that content from traditional publishers, they launched KDP Publishing to allow any writer, anywhere in the world, the ability to create and publish an ebook with no upfront costs. They decided to sweeten the deal by offering something no publisher would ever be able to do – authors publishing through KDP could keep 70% of the list price as royalty if they priced their book between $2.99-$9.99.

Early on, some enterprising authors realized their work could fill gaps in the ebook market for hungry readers. In 2010, Amanda Hocking decided to put her rejected paranormal YA books up for sale for $0.99 each, and 18 months later she'd sold 1.5 million copies. Midlist thriller author Joe Konrath started self-publishing his out-of-print titles and found himself moving 1,000 units a day. These authors wrote about their experiences online, and more and more authors joined KDP.

By 2011, ebooks were firmly established as part of the reading landscape. The New York Times added an ebook bestseller list in both fiction and non-fiction. Self-publishing success stories started to spread, and more authors jumped on board.

Amazon changed the market again in July 2014 by launching Kindle Unlimited, a subscription program where voracious readers could borrow an unlimited number of books each month for a flat fee – KU is Spotify for books. Instead of being paid a per-book royalty, authors with their books enrolled in KU are paid for every ebook page read.

All was great in the digital world... or was it? Readers rebelled against digital books and started buying expensive print books in droves. Or did they?

You might have seen articles in well-regarded publications like *The Guardian*, *Forbes*, and *Mental Floss*, explaining how digital books have fallen in popularity as readers lust after the bygone days of print. These articles make traditional publishers feel good. They are... sort of true. But also not true at all.

The writers of their pieces rely on data taken from Nielsen, who record book sales for each ISBN. That data shows that fewer people are reading digital books, as the sales of ISBNs on digital books have decreased. There's no denying that.

However, you don't need an ISBN to self-publish your books on Amazon. Many self-published authors don't use ISBNs because they can cost money and be a hassle to procure. Here in New Zealand, we get ours for free. In other countries, you pay as much as $100 per ISBN, and you need a new ISBN for each format. Self-publishing success is going unnoticed and uncounted by the wider industry, which means they struggle to react.

The data also doesn't cover a vast quantity of self-published books. The most comprehensive studies have been compiled by a site called Author Earnings, associated with the author Hugh Howey (another early self-publishing success story) and his data-loving friend known only as 'Data Guy.' Author Earnings has unfortunately disappeared from the internet, but many of the results are still available from secondary sources.

Author Earnings analyzed data about online book sales, including self-publishing stats as far as they can be extrapolated from publicly-available Amazon data. Their work showed 65% of fiction readers prefer reading digitally, that big 5 publishers account for only 18% of digital sales, and that self-publishers own 40% of the total ebook market. That's 40% of the market that isn't counted in Nielsen stats. Far from declining in popularity, this section of the digital market – the self-published books – **is growing and taking market share every year**.

Certain genres will always have a huge print market – coffee table books, children's picture books, literary fiction, etc – and it's important as an author and publisher to understand how people in your genre are reading your books. You may be surprised to learn that it's digitally.

Who is reading all these ebooks? Most self-publishing success stories are from genre fiction – crime, thrillers, romance, mysteries, horror, science fiction, and fantasy. If you're writing in one of these genres, you are already on the way to success. If not, don't fear – it may take a little bit more imagination and ingenuity, but there will be a way to find your readers.

SELF-PUBLISHING AND PRINT

While most successful self-published authors focus on genre fiction in ebook, some have found success with print.

Print success for indies (independent authors – another name for self-published authors) doesn't usually mean following the traditional model of finding a distributor and getting books into bookshops. Some do this, but it can be difficult to find a distributor who deals with indies, and if you do, they may require a large volume. Their discount plus the bookstore discount when combined with the higher per-unit price of POD books often means this is barely profitable for the author.

However, bookstores aren't the only place where readers buy print. Many of the most successful print-focused authors I know are public speakers or other figures who have established an audience.

Gala Darling (www.galadarling.com) is a blogger I've followed for years. Gala built a platform on her blog with her fun posts about fashion and creating outfits that made her smile. Over the years she pivoted from being a fashion blogger to talking about self-esteem and a concept she created called 'radical self-love.' She amassed a following of thousands of rabid readers. Before self-publishing through KDP was even a thing, Gala started writing a book about radical self love and releasing a chapter every month. Her readers could grab each chapter for $10 and get a PDF and an audio track of Gala reading the chapter aloud.

According to Gala, she made $100k selling her book in this way. She decided to edit the chapters together into a proper book and pitch it to publishers. She couldn't get anyone to offer her a deal, so she self-published *Radical Self Love* through KDP – she only had a paperback version available, but her fans snapped it up and sent her soaring to the top of the self-help and metaphysical categories. Her success caught the attention of Hay House, who offered her a publishing deal.

What's unusual about Gala's story is that she didn't even self-publish an ebook version of *Radical Self Love*. She knew most of her loyal readers had those early chapters stashed on their hard-drive, and wanted to push them to a physical product. Gala's self-publishing experiment worked because she spent years building her audience online. Gala has since self-published more books and almanacs and recently launched a print magazine. Gala's story shows how powerful an engaged audience can be, and the power of constantly creating new and useful things for that audience.

I know a great number of authors who've had success launching books via crowdfunding on Kickstarter. Usually, these are books that can be given as gifts – children's books, art/photography books, or journals. Often they have a geeky theme or focus on some niche area in the book industry where traditional publishers won't touch.

Have you ever heard of Littlest Lovecraft? (www.facebook.com/littlestlovecraft) They're two artists who created children's picture books based on H. P. Lovecraft's cosmic horror stories. They are freaking adorable, but this is something a publisher never would have picked up. But by taking their books straight to Kickstarter, they were able to find an audience. Each of their five Kickstarter campaigns has raised between $25-45,000.

Also on the Lovecraft theme, I picked up a cookbook called the Necronomnomnom from Kickstarter (www.reddukegames.com). This was a cookbook designed to look like an ancient magical tome, complete with calligraphy and esoteric doodles on every page. It's as much a piece of art as it is a cookbook, and it appealed to the geeky audience of Kickstarter, who backed it to $80,000. For a project like this, readers want to own the print version (and sometimes even the deluxe limited edition version) and will pay a premium for the privilege.

And let us not overlook one of the most popular Kickstarters of all time – *Goodnight Stories for Rebel Girls* (www.rebelgirls.com). The authors started off creating apps and app magazines for kids, but after the market slowed, they worked with a traditional publisher on a series of six picture books. This series didn't go as well as the authors anticipated, but they loved creating books, so they decided to focus on publishing themselves through their own company, Timbuktu Labs, and to focus on building their audience online. They brought a lot of knowledge from the start-up world to build their community and market their books.

Their books telling inspiring stories of real women in a fairy-tale format have sold more than 3 million copies. Read more about the authors and their thought-process around the books here.

Other areas where print can do well:

- Any book you can sell at events you're already involved in, such as art books for gallery shows, comic books and graphic novels for cons, and professional speakers selling books at the back of the room.
- Adult coloring books. Collect 20 related original line images together and publish on thick paper.
- Poetry books that reach a specific audience. Many poets sell print copies and chapbooks at events and build a community on social media to push their books.
- Creating your own magazine/workbook. For example, Kat Williams of Rock N Roll Bride

(www.rocknrollbride.com) self-publishes her own glossy bridal magazine based on her blog content.

- Limited edition hardback versions of your books for collectors, perhaps including special paper types, embossed covers, or illustrations.

THE FUTURE OF SELF-PUBLISHING IS WIDE OPEN

Every day I read or listen to stories of self-published authors finding their readers and seeing success. This industry hasn't even scratched the surface of what technology and innovation will make possible in years to come.

The only question you have to ask yourself is whether you want to join us in the trenches. Are you ready for the wild ride of publishing your own work and taking your stories to the world?

Enough of my rambling – let's get into it!

Chapter Four

STEP 1. FIGURE OUT WHAT SELF-PUBLISHING SUCCESS MEANS TO YOU

What are you trying to achieve with self-publishing?

Answering this question impacts every subsequent decision you make about your writing, from what book to write and which distributors to choose, to how and where to market. Are you:

- Wanting to disseminate information and ideas, or raise your profile within your industry? (By writing a non-fiction book on your topic of expertise).
- Producing a family history book? (To chronicle the lives of your ancestors for posterity).
- Using a book as an additional tool to showcase your other creative work? (For example, a photographer compiling their work into a tabletop art book. A chef creating a cookbook to sell at their cafe).
- Breaking into a new market? (A commercial illustrator producing their first children's book).
- Wanting a physical product to sell at events? (If you're a motivational speaker or poet).

- Fulfilling a lifelong dream to tell wonderful stories?
- Using publishing as a motivation tool to force yourself to finish your writing projects?
- Writing for creative pleasure and to see a copy of your book on the shelf?
- Wanting to write books and make a little extra money on the side of your day job?
- Trying to make a full-time living as an author?

Every one of these reasons is totally valid and completely achievable. There's no value judgment on who you are or what you want out of your writing. We're talking about this now because you gotta know your own **metric for success** before you dive in.

Why? Because this book is all about rocking self-publishing – i.e. being successful. But 'success' is a nebulous term that means completely new things to different writers. Every section of this book is designed to give you ideas to build your own rocking plan, and you can't build a plan if you don't know what 'success' is.

An author who wants to publish their family history will have a completely different idea of success to the writer who wants to quit their day job. The artist who wants to create a quality book for their collectors will have a different approach from the fantasy author who wants to pitch their series to Netflix.

My approach for this book deals particularly with getting your writing to as many people as possible and making a living as a self-published author. This was my primary goal when I started pursuing publishing ten years ago, and that's the goal of most of the peeps in my Rage Against The Manuscript group (www.facebook.com/groups/rageagainst-themanuscript.com). In saying that, many of the techniques and ideas will work just as well no matter your endgame. I just want you to be aware if you're feeling overwhelmed that my success metric is different from yours, and that's okay.

Only you can decide your measure of success. It's most likely obvious to you, as it's the driving force behind your innate *need* to write. No one is forcing you to work on this writing project instead of watching TV, so why are you doing it? Because you have a story inside you burning to get out? Because you think other people would find your information useful? Because your fans/followers/customers have been asking for it? Because you believe your writing will create a better life for your family? Because you want to change the world? A combination of all of these?

Answer the why and you'll arrive at the heart of your measure of success.

A lot of people burn out from their creative pursuits because they don't ask themselves what brings them joy. I know this from personal experience.

I enjoy drawing and painting, and although I've never been professionally trained, I do have some skills. In my 20s, I tried to set myself up as an illustrator. I thought it would be a great sideline to writing and help me to land more work. So I spent my evenings creating pieces for an illustration portfolio, working on a children's book, and reading articles about being a professional illustrator. I even started pitching myself to some publishers and had a bit of interest.

It was fun, for a while. Then it started to feel like things weren't happening fast enough. That it was too hard. One day I found I couldn't bear to sit in front of the easel any longer. The idea of painting *repulsed* me. I resented the fledgling sideline I'd built for myself. I thought all my work sucked. I wanted to tear my drawings up and never show them to anyone ever again.

I'd taken the joy out of drawing because I'd never sat down to ask myself *why* I liked to draw. And when I did that soul-searching, I discovered that I had no desire to draw commercially for clients based on *their* briefs. I liked doodling things that made me smile. I found satisfaction from completing a drawing, from mastering new skills, from hanging a painting on the wall in our home or giving it away as a gift. But I didn't want to run an online store and deal with bad reviews and a social media presence and limited print runs and pitching for publishers. That wasn't fun to me because I'd let my real passion – writing – dry up amongst all that other stuff.

Don't let this happen with your writing.

I'm a big believer that your creative pursuits should be insanely, joyously *fun*. They should make you excited to get home in the evening, they should occupy your thoughts in the shower, they should be a celebration of who you are and what you stand for. There are literally a million easier ways of making a living than following a creative career. That's a fact – a million easier ways to make them sweet dolla bills. I'll count them for if you want to wait.

No? You sure?

Let's say I'm right. There are lots of easier ways to make a living. Not all of them will be enjoyable, but if the end goal is riches, who cares? *You* care – because you want to write. Because writing and telling stories is fun.

Why pursue a writing career with no guarantees of fame and fortune if it's not fun?

Some of us enjoy the creative challenge of simply finishing a project. Others are lit up by creating something for their existing fans or presenting their current creative passions in a new way. You might be drawn to the rush and validation of winning contests and prizes, or you have ideas and stories you want as many people to enjoy as possible. You might be like me and you want to create a body of work that makes me proud and offers something good to the world. Also, like me, writing might be the only thing you want to do all day and you enjoy the challenge of building your income to a point where you can quit your job.

Look at the writing and other activities you already do in your spare time. What occupies your thoughts? What excites you and fires up your imagination? What do you work on when no one is forcing you to work? This is where you'll find what you're truly passionate about.

Think of what you're really trying to achieve with your project. What lights you up?

- I want to see my book in print.
- I want to create something I'm proud of.
- I want to create a fun product that my followers/fans/customers will love.
- I want to win literary prizes and awards.
- I want 20,000 people to read my book.
- I want to see my book on the shelves in bookstores and libraries.
- I want to spread ideas/stories that will change the world.
- I want to help pay the bills with my writing.
- I want to make a full-time living from my writing.

Now that you know your own success metrics, if possible, put some solid numbers on it. What's your timeline? What numbers are meaningful to you? If you want to finish your family history, then your goal could be to complete research by the end of the year and have a first draft completed by next July.

If your dream is to make a living as a writer, what does that mean? What monthly income do you have to hit? When do you want to hit it? Figure that out and start building a plan to work toward it. For me, when I set this goal, I wanted to earn 75% of my current salary, and I had a year to do it. I'll tell that story a little later in the book.

I'm not going to do a whole chapter on SMART goals, because we've all heard the lecture and we know the acronym – but you should be making your writing success goals as SMART as possible. If you want a refresher, there's a great article about SMART goals for writers on the *Happy Self-Publisher* (http://happyselfpublisher.com/smart-goals-for-writers/).

LITERARY ACCLAIM OR A MILLION DOLLARS?

The book world is firmly divided down the middle into two separate teams. A select few books occupy a nebulous space somewhere in the middle, but they're the exception. Most of us sit firmly on one side or another.

Literary: According to *The Guardian*, "Literary writers are the luxury brands of the writing world... these people are smarter than you, so you should buy their book." (https://www.theguardian.com/books/books-blog/2015/nov/20/literature-vs-genre-is-a-battle-where-both-sides-lose). Literary fiction is often introspective and focuses on wider issues important to humanity. Its purpose is to make you think. Literary fiction is what ends up on award lists and taught on a university syllabus. (I include most poetry in the literary category).

Commercial/Genre: This is what the majority of people read. These are books to scratch an itch – familiar stories and characters that make you happy. Although genre fiction can and does tackle the world and the human condition, its primary purpose is to entertain. Genre fiction includes crime and thrillers, science fiction and fantasy, historical, and romance.

Generally speaking, if you seek acclaim, then you go in

the literary direction. If you want money, you want to think about genre. You can think about non-fiction writing similarly. There's non-fiction written for acclaim, and non-fiction written to entertain and inform. There's no value judgment here – you have to decide for yourself where your talent and passion lie.

Also, generally speaking, genre fiction will do better self-published. This is because genre readers don't make as many value judgments about *the publisher of a book* as literary readers. Genre readers choose books that look entertaining from their preferred category, whereas literary readers rely more heavily on reviews from certain publications, award lists (that won't accept self-published work), and the quality standard of their favorite publishers to make their buying decisions.

If you're a genre writer, self-publishing has great potential to help you reach your dreams. If you're writing non-fiction that entertains and informs, you're also in a great position as people looking for information don't tend to care where it comes from and how it's delivered as long as it's engaging and answers their questions.

If you believe you're a literary writer, then think carefully about your goals and success metrics and whether self-publishing is the right way to reach your readers. It's definitely possible, but it's going to be hard work, and you've got to laser-focus on your readers' habits and preferences.

HOW TO ROCK YOUR SUCCESS METRICS:

- What does success as a writer mean for you?
- Imagine yourself five years from now. (If this feels too difficult, narrow down to one year from now). Picture yourself as a writer. What does that look like? How many books have you published? What

genre? Do you write full time? Are you selling
poetry books at an event? Who are your readers?
What does your writing contribute to the world?
What have you created? How do you feel about
your career? Describe your dreams and vision in
the past tense, as if it's already happened. Knowing
where you want to be will help you see where you
should focus.

- What have you already done to move toward that
  dream? Make a list of all the projects you've
  completed or are half-finished on your hard drive.
  What about writing groups or social networks you
  participate in? Awards you've won? Craft books
  you've read? Look at this list for patterns and
  proclivities.
- What's an immediate goal that will get you closer
  to your ideal future? Is it finishing a book,
  publishing a project, launching a new pen name, or
  creating an author brand?
- Are you a literary writer or a genre writer?

Chapter Five

STEP 2. YOU NEED MORE THAN ONE BOOK

Here's the thing – books hit the market with gusto. They get lots of attention during their first few months of publication, and then reader interest wanes as soon as more shiny new books hit the shelves.

If you want a sustainable long term career as an author, you need more than one book. The more new releases you have, the more you'll get to hit that 'new release spike' and capture more fans who'll go back to buy all your previous books.

There are exceptions, of course. Harper Lee made her career from a single book. But I always choose not to believe I'll be the exception.

(As I said previously, I wrote this book based on my experiences and my personal success metric – which was to become a full-time author and make enough to pay the mortgage and keep my cats in the manner to which they've become accustomed. If that's not your goal then some of these tips may not apply to you, especially this one).

In indie publishing, you only have to sell 1,000 books a month with a $3.99 price tag to make an average wage (average here in New Zealand, anyway). You'll earn a 70%

royalty for each book sold at that price-point, so you can do the math to see how many books you'd need to sell each month in order to pay your bills. Don't forget to also factor in taxes, health insurance, and a savings cushion!

For an average person, I estimate the magic number for a sustainable career is around 1,000 books per month. That may seem like a huge number to hit if you only have one book (especially as that book will fall in popularity over time), but when you have 5 or 10 or 20 books in your backlist, your 1k-book target becomes achievable. Add audiobooks and paperbacks and other income streams, and you'll be rocking your way to the bank.

Instead of imagining your one book hitting bestseller lists and paying for a fancy mansion (or even just a studio apartment these days), think about what you want your career as an author to look like. What kind of books do you want to be known for? How will they all fit together? Will you write for kids or adults? Are you a commercial or literary writer? Do you write series or standalones? If a reader was talking about you to someone, how would they describe you?

This is what people talk about when they talk about your 'author brand.' It can help to distill your brand down into a simple sentence that describes what you do. For example, my brand for Steffanie Holmes is 'paranormal romance with a touch of the gothic.' Every book I write under that pen name fits in some way into that brand, as does any promotion I run or social media post I make. I always want readers to be able to pick up one of my books and visit one of my homes on the internet and know what to expect.

I also have another pen name – Steff Green – and that has a different, non-romance brand. I use two pen names because the projects appeal to a different audience, although I do cross-promote them.

You don't have to do this 'branding' exercise if that kind

of thing gives you hives. It's just useful to have a sense of where you're going so you can get excited about your future projects and direction. Also, being consistent with what you give your audience will help you to build a sustainable career and reach your success metrics sooner.

AUTHOR BRANDING

Talking about 'branding' can feel really corporate and boring. And after I did that big spiel about how I believe your writing career should always be fun!

I know, I know, but branding is an important thing to get a grip on if you want to make a career of this or if you're writing books as part of a wider strategy. Besides, it is kind of fun. It's basically a thought exercise in how to distill the essence of YOU into a fun little package.

Branding isn't a logo. It isn't a website or a style guide. Branding is **making and keeping a promise to your audience**. Good branding says, "you can trust me. I promise I'm going to give you exactly what you want every single time."

A solid brand is why people return to fast food restaurants like McDonald's again and again. You know that no matter what city you're in anywhere in the world, you can walk into a McDonald's and purchase the exact same thing and it will taste identical. It's trustworthy in a world where very few things feel dependable.

You already have an author brand. You don't even have to do anything! Because a brand isn't something that you *do* – it's the way people see you and how you make them feel. People already make judgments about you and your work based on what you put out in the world. Now that you know this, you can take control. The way you package your books, your words, and yourself will enable you to influence the brand you want.

Your brand is a billboard telling the world who you are and what you stand for. It allows other people who enjoy the same things and agree with what you stand for to easily identify you. Actively tweaking and controlling your brand gives you the power to find and attract these readers.

You may think it's too early to be thinking about this stuff. It depends. On what? **On your success metrics.** If you're trying to publish a memoir so you have something to give your grandma for Christmas, your brand doesn't matter so much. If you want to be a full-time successful self-published author, then your brand matters a hell of a lot. The sooner you nail a consistent brand, the sooner you can put the other tips in this book into action.

So how do you create your author brand?

The first step is to understand who you're writing for. Who are your readers? What are their likes and dislikes? How old are they, where do they live, and what gender do they identify as? How many books do they read in a month, and how do they like to read them? The more you know about your readers, the better you can craft your brand and your books to fit their desires.

Knowing this stuff doesn't mean you have to hire a market research firm or tarot card reader. For some genres, there's already reader demographic information available. Just search online and you'll find lots of great info about reading habits. If you can't find anything, you'll need to dig around to uncover what you need. Look at blogs, discussion boards, and reader groups for books in your genre. Check out the reviews on a popular book – how much demographic information can you glean from those? Talk to readers of your genre and develop a small survey (www.SurveyMonkey.com is great for these). Look at authors you love and how they use their brands to appeal to certain types of readers.

Once you know who you're talking to, you need to figure

out what you want your brand to say to them. How do they like to be spoken to? What words and imagery appeal and what is a huge turn-off. Look at how other authors speak to their readers and take lessons to apply to your own brand. We call this 'brand voice.'

Penny Reid (www.pennyreid.ninja) is a great example of an author brand. Her books are romantic comedy for women. Everything about her public persona speaks to this brand. Her book covers convey the genre and tone. Even if you took her name away, they're instantly recognizable as Penny Reid covers. Her tone on her website and social media is bright and breezy and funny. You won't see her going off on a political rant. She doesn't suddenly surprise readers with a dark noir suspense book or a romantic hero who dies at the end – readers know what to expect when they pick up her work. That's why they love her.

Think about what you want readers to expect from your brand. Going back to the earlier example, when we go to McDonald's, we know exactly what to expect. It's not gourmet fare, but it has a taste all of its own, and that familiarity is comforting. What can readers expect from you? How long will your books be? Will they be series or standalone? How often will they come out? Will you work on multiple series at once or finish them one at a time? How much access will they have to you via social media? How will they be notified when you put out a new book? Will your brand encompass projects that aren't writing?

No matter how you decide to brand yourself, part of your brand should always be to put out books of high quality, with excellent editing, that are joyful to read. We'll talk a bit more about this later.

WRITERS AND PEN NAMES

Your pen name – whether it's your real name or something invented – is the keystone of your brand. It's how readers recognize you. The tighter the brand of your pen name and the books you publish under it, the more sell-through you'll get from one book to the next, and the faster you'll get to that magic 1,000 books a month. We're going to talk more about sell-through later. For now, think about how you will tie your books together under a pen name.

We've talked about how a consistent brand is important, and how readers like to rely on you giving them the same kind of story. What if you want to write lots of different things? You want to write historical romance! And cookbooks! And dog-walking manuals! And YA fantasy! You have three options:

1. You can throw everything you do up **under one pen name** and hope that some readers will like everything and the rest won't get annoyed at the lack of consistency. The advantage of this is that you only have one pen name to deal with, and you can use covers and titles to clearly indicate genre. The main problem with it is that when a reader looks at your backlist, they'll feel confused by all the different options. They don't know what they're getting. They will be less likely to read through other books you've written than if you stuck tight with one genre. Also, you'll probably struggle to gain traction in Amazon's algorithms because it will be difficult for the bots to understand what you write and who will want to read it.

2. You can separate out each different genre into a

new pen name or identity. You might put your cookbooks under one pen name and your romance under another and your YA fiction under a third name. The advantage here is you'll have tighter branding and higher sell-through on each pen name. The disadvantage is that you'll have to manage multiple pen names, publishing schedules, marketing, and social media profiles. It will be tough to keep up, and inevitably, you'll end up favoring some names over others. You'll probably see slower progress then if you focused on one single name and genre.

3. You can find ways to tweak your concepts and interests to **incorporate passion projects under one main pen name.** For example, if you have a historical romance series where the heroine is a cook for a fancy estate, perhaps you could create a cookbook based on the series to sell to fans. The advantage is that you can have fun doing all the creative things you enjoy while building a strong, dedicated fanbase that knows what to expect. The disadvantage is that you might not be doing exactly what you want in the way you want it.

3 is the option I strive for because I want to avoid spreading myself thin across multiple pen names if at all possible. I've followed this in my own career. For years I've wanted to write a mystery series – specifically, a cozy or traditional mystery set in small-town England. Doing so would mean starting an entirely new pen name, and I didn't want to do that. Instead, I wrote the Nevermore Bookshop Mysteries series – mashing up the mystery format with a steamy reverse harem romance plot. I got to write my mystery series without

having to start a new pen name. When I released it, it became my most popular series to date.

Another author who does this really well is historical author Libbie Hawker (www.hawkerbooks.com). Historical authors are usually branding according to the era they write in, but Libbie has been able to indulge her passion for multiple historical periods through her brand – often by focusing on periods and historical personalities that aren't well-covered by other historical writers. Libbie's work might appeal to a smaller audience, but she's able to dominate underserved niches and respond to trending reader interests.

HOW TO ROCK YOUR AUTHOR BRAND:

- Your brand isn't about a book. It's about YOU and the way you make your readers feel. Branding is attached to your author name and encompasses not just the books you publish under that name, but your entire author presence both off- and online.
- You already have an author brand. Branding is the images and associations created in a reader's mind when they hear your name. With a little work and strategic thinking, you can control that brand to be in line with your **success metrics**.
- Can you sum up your brand in a single sentence? You don't have to tell anyone the sentence, but thinking about your brand as a simple catch-phrase can help you to quickly assess if a decision is on-brand for you or not.
- Who are your readers? Know them and design your brand to appeal to them.
- How will your brand help you to get to your ideal

author career? Look at how other authors in your genre manage their brands. Don't stop at visual cues like logos and cover fonts – look at how they speak to readers, how they set a publishing schedule, what they talk about on social media, and most importantly – how their brand makes readers *feel*.

- Pen names – will you have one? How many will you use? How will you manage each name and what will each brand contribute to your success?

Chapter Six

STEP 3. CONSIDER A SERIES

As a self-published author, you wear three hats. I think they're quite trendy hats, but then, I do like hats.

You wear your **writer hat** to get the words on paper. This is a super-creative hat that may not be very good at keeping the rain off, but it will definitely turn heads if you wear it around town.

Once the book is finished you have to take that hat off and put on your **publisher hat** and your **marketing hat**. Your publisher hat is safe and boring, but it keeps your head warm and is super comfy. Your marketing hat is trendy and fashionable and sophisticated and perfectly compliments your outfit. However, you brought it on a whim and it probably cost a bit more than you're used to. You don't trust your marketing hat. It seems too ostentatious, too *out there*. Donning it makes you a bit nervous because it's not something you'd normally wear, but as soon as you step out, people exclaim over how awesome it looks.

(The more you wear your marketing hat, the more comfortable it gets. One day you won't even remember feeling nervous about it at all).

All this talk of hats is just my roundabout way of explaining if you're going to self-publish, as well as being an awesome writer you are now also your own publishing house *and* the marketing department of that publishing house. Most of us don't know how to do either of those things.

Becoming a publisher is the easier bit. You get a free account on Amazon KDP or Kobo Writing Life or whichever platforms you like, follow the steps, and at the end, you have a book!

But when it comes to marketing, you probably feel a little overwhelmed. Most of us haven't marketed a product in our lives, much less a book containing our heart and soul and at least three of our organs. Later in this guide, we'll talk about how to market your published book. Right now, I'm sharing a little secret about how to plan for success with your marketing before you write a single word.

Truth time – a series of connected books in the same world is much easier to market than standalone stories.

Why? Sell-through. Readers become invested in the characters and stakes in book one. A certain percentage of those readers go on to buy book two, and a certain percentage of *those* readers will buy books three and four and so on. Using this model, if you get enough people to read book one – even if you **lose money marketing that book** – you can make a profit on the people who progress through the series.

Indie authors like me can calculate our sell-through on a series and see which books perform better than others, or if there's something making readers put down a series before the end. When I release a series, I expect to see around 50% sell-through to book 2 (half the readers who finish book 1 will pick up book 2), 50-60% sell-through to book 3, and then **90-95% sell-through** from book 3 onward. This means if you're making enough money from each launch in a series, you can keep adding as many new books as you like and you'll know roughly how many sales to expect.

Bestselling romance author Bella Andre (www.bellaandre.-com) uses this logic. She's been writing her Sullivans series since the start of her career. She's now sold over 8 million books with over 20 titles in the series. She knows that if she keeps putting out Sullivans she'll have a guaranteed number of readers for each new release.

Sell-through is much harder on standalone books. Readers have to become invested in a brand new set of characters every time. Readers are series loyal first and foremost, which is why many readers will only read the most popular series by an author and not their other works. Not everyone who read the Harry Potter books also read JK Rowling's 2012 tragicomedy *The Casual Vacancy* (even if they consider Rowling one of their favorite authors).

There are other advantages to writing in series. Sales platforms like Amazon and Apple Books help to promote your series by making sure readers are alerted to the next book. You can bundle series books together into a boxset, which is a great way to draw in new readers. Box-sets are an effective marketing tool because they command a higher price point (for example, you might combine 3 books that retail for $3.99 into a $9.99 boxset) and only require one sale instead of three.

Having a series also makes it really easy to establish your author brand, as the series title and cohesive covers quickly establish you as a particular type of author.

TYPES OF SERIES

Series work well for fiction, non-fiction, and even poetry. There are many different types of series you could try. I've invented some fun titles so you can remember the different types.

EPIC SERIES (WITH CLIFFHANGERS)

An epic series is where you basically split one giant-ass story into several books. Each book follows the same cast of characters through their trials and perils. The tension and stakes will usually increase in each book so that by the end of the series you've got some kind of epic showdown.

Each book in your epic series should have a satisfying arc that answers some of the questions raised during the book, even if the story itself continues. If you're clever, you'll end each book in your epic on a cliffhanger to entice readers to continue. Readers will often say "I hate cliffhangers," but their behavior says otherwise. If you use cliffhangers in your series you will usually have better sell-through (and more moolah!), but poorer reviews. Up to you which one you prefer.

Some examples of epic books are *The Hunger Games* by Suzanne Collins, *The Lord of the Rings* by J. R. R. Tolkien, and my own Briarwood Witches and Kings of Miskatonic Prep series.

THE BAND OF BROTHERS SERIES

This is the series format most commonly employed by romance writers, but I've seen it in other genres, too. I've named it a Band of Brothers because although each book would include a new romantic pairing, one member of that pairing (usually the guy in MF romance – but they don't have to be men!) is part of a close group of other characters – this might be a family group (actual brothers), or it might be a wolf pack, a law firm, a football team, a motorcycle club... the possibilities are endless.

This series format enables you to introduce the other 'brothers' (connected characters – not necessarily men) in the first book so the readers get hooked on them and *need* to know how their stories turn out. Often, but not always, a Band of Brothers series will have an overarching storyline or mystery that will stretch across multiple books, but the responsibility for finding the next clue in the mystery will be passed to the new POV characters.

Bella Andre uses the Band of Brothers format for her popular Sullivans series, as does pretty much every other romance author. JA Huss creates an interesting Band of Brothers dynamic in her Turning dark romance series, where three rich friends keep a string of women locked in a dark room. I use this series type in my Crookshollow Gothic Romance and Wolves of Crookshollow series, but I now prefer to follow the same characters across multiple books.

THE ADVENTURES OF... SERIES

In this series format, you meet the main character in book one, where they will have an adventure that will be neatly wrapped up by the end of book one. In book two, they'll begin another adventure.

Readers continue to devour The Adventures Of... books not because they need to know what happens, but because they're obsessed with the main character and the world you've created.

This is the most popular series format for mystery and thriller books. Think about Kathy Reichs – her books are standalone stories, but they're connected by the main character or set in the same location. There may also be an overarching series arc, but it will usually move much slower than other series types.

Another of my favorite authors who rocks this format is cozy mystery writer H. Y. Hanna. I've not only fallen in love with her main (female) protagonists, but also the delightful settings and a cast of quirky characters she uses to populate her worlds.

I also use this format in my Nevermore Bookshop Mysteries series, although I do also employ mild cliffhangers to keep the ongoing mystery alive.

TUNE IN NEXT WEEK SERIALS

Serials are a very specific type of fiction – usually written like the book form of a TV show. They're released in short installments on a regular schedule – usually a few days or a week apart. Readers know exactly when they can expect a new episode, and they enjoy reading a short part of a story in on go.

During the Victorian Penny Dreadful era where many people got their fiction fix from short fiction, serials were a popular format. Charles Dickens made his name writing serials. They fell out of favor as reading habits changed and readers could purchase more lengthy works cheaply.

Thanks to digital reading, serials are seeing a resurgence. Readers are now less tied to considering the length of a book when they choose what to read, and the low price points of digital books make purchasing individual episodes of a serial (or reading them in Kindle Unlimited) affordable.

Popular self-published series have included H. M. Ward's Arrangement series, Luke Jennings' *Codename Villanelle*, and Sean Platt's work. Serials usually won't do as well as full-length novels (there are fewer readers interested in the format) but many serial writers find they do quite well if they release regularly, particularly when they bundle episodes into boxsets readers can binge at once.

TRUST ME – I KNOW WHAT I'M TALKING ABOUT SERIES (NON-FICTION)

You may be thinking, "these series ideas are all well and good, Steff, but what about if I write non-fiction?"

As a non-fiction writer, you can still take advantage of the power of the series.

If you write narrative non-fiction or memoir, then understand that in terms of plot and marketing (if not content), these act in the same way as a fiction series. It's common for narrative non-fiction to be presented as a series and the use of cliffhangers and other tools to encourage readers to pick up future books. Jean Sasson's *Princess* books are a classic example.

If your books don't fit this model, you can still use series branding. Think about overarching ideas or themes that will spread across all of your books. Can you group your books together into topics that would appeal to the same type of person?

A great example of non-fiction series branding is Tim Ferriss, author of bestselling book, *The 4-Hour Workweek*. Tim developed a unique way of running a business and managing his time so that he only had to work four hours a week. When he released his next book, *The 4-Hour Body*, he took a subject matter that was completely different and framed it within his same formula to create a natural progression between the two books. He used the same branding to promote *The 4-Hour Body* and a subsequent book *The 4-Hour Chef* to his existing audience.

THE PRETTY BOOKSHELF: POETRY SERIES

"Okay, sure, but riddle me this!" I hear you cry. "I'm a *poet*. How do I create a series for poetry? Do I even need a series?"

To which I reply, you don't need a series. Because these aren't rules – they are guidelines to help you rock self-publishing. But as you've learned, a series is a great way to make your life easier in terms of marketing your work, building lifelong fans, and selling more books.

A poetry series works differently to other books. If you create epic poems in a saga format you could create an ongoing series narrative (The *Odyssey* was the sequel to the *Iliad*, after all). But probably most poets aren't doing that and most poetry readers aren't looking for that experience. (I don't know – maybe they are! You gotta find out).

The key comes in thinking about who your readers are and why they like to buy poetry. Poetry lovers enjoy beautiful language that evokes a place or time or feeling. They also adore the aesthetic joy of words and books as objects. Poetry is among the few self-published genres where the majority of your readers will want a print copy. They want to put it on their shelf and admire it as an *objet d'art*.

More than any other genre, a poetry book should be a pleasure to hold. Look at self-publishing options that allow for different paper and binding types. You could perhaps consider hardback or linen. You may like to do a cheaper version and a deluxe edition with a higher price point for collectors.

Can you find ways to thematically join your collections? Use series branding to create a cohesive look. Your readers will feel as though they need to collect all the books. Also, group poems into collections by type and link the titles together in a similar way. Look at how publishers sell poetry collections as a series and borrow inspiration.

As you'll probably sell a lot of print books at poetry slams and readings, consider doing a small print run locally as well as a POD version for online sales. You can do both versions with the same ISBN number.

For some more great advice about self-publishing poetry, check out this article with ten tips by poet Christine Mokoginta (https://www.magloft.com/blog/self-publishing-poetry).

HOW TO ROCK WRITING IN A SERIES:

- Can you find a way to pivot your current project to be a series?
- What series types are most popular in your genre?
- Look at how other authors use branding to link books into a series. Cover, blurbs, themes, tropes, subtitles, characters, settings... how you can learn from their success? What branding elements can you incorporate into your series?
- To cliffhanger or not to cliffhanger, that is the question.

Chapter Seven

STEP 4. RELEASE AS OFTEN AS POSSIBLE

If you are trying to make a living as an author or get the most eyes on your work, then the more often you release something new, the more opportunity you give yourself to earn a livable income.

If you pursue traditional publishing, your publisher will probably only want to release one book by you per year. Research into reader habits has led publisher to adopt this strategy – believing that more than this means your books are competing against themselves for readers' money. Also, publishers only have a limited amount of resources to dedicate to each author. Books are expensive and readers only have so much fun money, and your publisher doesn't want them to have to choose between two of your titles.

You might be able to get two publishing deals from different publishers and release two books in a year, but those books will be in different series and you may run into problems with non-compete clauses in your contracts.

The rise of digital reading and cheap ebook prices means that voracious readers can devour many more books per month than they could afford to when print was their only option. This explains the success of Amazon's Kindle Unlimited – the 'Spotify for books' where readers pay $10 per month to read as many books enrolled in the program as they like. (You'll be learning about Kindle Unlimited in excruciating detail later).

This lower average list price has brought out what the industry likes to call 'whale' readers. These are voracious bibliophiles who read 1-2 books a *day*. Because of the high price of print books, they're used to relying on libraries to fuel their desire for more books, all the time. Now, they're able to purchase more titles outright.

Most whale readers quickly made the switch to digital reading as soon as Amazon improved the selection available. They tend to obsessively stick to a single genre, and they love Kindle Unlimited. They don't care whether a book is self-published or traditionally-published as long as it's entertaining and hits the tropes.

In genres where these 'whale' readers hang out – which tend to be the commercial genres such as thrillers, mysteries, romance, science fiction, fantasy, and women's fiction – self-published writers are making a killing by publishing often with low prices.

We also make higher sell-through because if a reader is devouring two books per day, in a year they will have forgotten your first book. But if I can give them the next installment in a couple of months they'll be so happy and excited.

Because self-published authors keep a high percentage of our royalties (70% on books priced between $2.99-9.99 on Amazon, as opposed to 10-25% off net in a traditional contract) we can afford to price low. Because we're only paying ourselves and we have low overheads (no office space to rent or staff salaries to manage), we can bank most of that as profit. A self-publishing success often looks the same as a traditionally-published failure (most big publishing houses need to sell 50,000 copies of a book to make a decent profit. If I sell 3,000 copies of a book, I make over $10k. To a traditional publisher, 3,000 books sold wouldn't even earn out an advance.)

As I've said before, you only have to sell 1,000 books a month with a $3.99 price tag to make an average wage. That may seem like a huge number of sales to achieve if you only have one book, but when you have 5 or 10 or 20 books (your backlist) the target becomes totally reachable. The quicker you create a backlist, the quicker you can earn big.

Also, if you release more often, you don't have to sell as many books with each release to create a viable career. If each book you release sells around 3,000-5,000 copies, one book per year will have you in the poorhouse, but what about 2-10 books per year? You can see how many self-publishers have thriving careers.

This is why many self-published authors have made successful careers in sub-genres and niche audiences traditional publishers won't touch. A higher profit per book means we can create a viable career from smaller numbers. Authors who write successfully in a niche can also build a dedicated following of fans who are desperate for stories traditional publishers can't give them. We're going to be talking about niches all through this book.

(An aside: How do you pronounce niche? I've always said 'neesh' but I've heard so many writers say 'nitch.' That makes my teeth grate, but I'm curious about your thoughts. Discuss).

One great example of self-published authors rocking a niche is the fiction genre of LitRPG (Literary Role-Playing Games). Portal fiction into a game world has been big for decades, and the modern genre of LitRPG came out of Russia, and went mainstream with a successful traditionally-published book – *Ready Player One* by Ernest Cline. But self-published authors have made the genre their own. The books read like the actual experience of leveling-up in a video game – you beat up monsters and baddies, grow your experience, and acquire better gear (and usually, a harem of lusty wenches). LitRPG has a growing fanbase of gamers who enjoy these books, but its generally not something a traditional publisher looking for the next bestseller will publish as the audience is small.

HOW TO RELEASE FAST

The release schedules of some authors can seem insane. Cozy mystery writer Amanda M. Lee and teen paranormal writer Bella Forrest both release a full-length novel every week. I'm currently writing and publishing a book every 4-6 weeks.

Don't let those numbers scare you. No one is saying you have to do that to succeed. Plenty of authors make a decent living and grow their audience publishing 3-4 books a year. That's only writing around 750 words per day.

Maybe even hearing '3-4 books per year' sounds terrifying. Maybe you've been fiddling with your novel for five years already. Maybe you think it's impossible you could ever find more time to write and increase your speed. I'm here to tell you that it's 100% possible, and something you should consider doing if you want to succeed as a self-publisher.

Writing is like a muscle – the more you exercise it, the stronger it becomes. It took me five years to write my first novel. And that was dedicating a ton of time each week to butt-in-chair writing. The next I wrote in two years. The next, six months. Now I can write and publish a novel in a month. The more you write, the more you learn about your working and publishing process. After a few books, you have it down to a finely tuned machine.

If you want to learn to write faster, there are a few things you can do:

CARVE OUT MORE WRITING TIME

You have a job, a family, kids, hobbies, charity work, other commitments. We all do. Finding time to write amongst all that can be tough.

If you want it bad enough, you will do it. Why? Cuz if you're a writer, then writing is the most fun you could imagine. If you're not feeling energized and excited about writing at least some of the time, then I'm not sure I can help you (a bit more on that later).

All things being equal, basic math suggests that if you have more time to write, you'll get more written. That's not strictly true because of reasons we'll get into, but it can be true. It's definitely worth giving it a go.

Think about where in your day you might be able to fit in some time. Can you go somewhere quiet for 20 minutes on your lunch break? Do you have an hour at the end of the day before the kids get home from school? Can you get up earlier and write before the rest of the house wakes up?

Over the years, I became somewhat of an expert at fitting in writing around my day job and other commitments. I don't have kids and I'm not looking after elderly relatives, so keep that in mind. I'd write on my lunch break. I'd write in the evenings. I'd get up early on weekends and write before my husband arose and started cooking bacon. In my final year of working a day job, I would write hunched over my laptop on the bus to/from my tech startup job. I'm not going to lie – it kind of sucked, but it enabled me to work that super-intense job with the horrendous commute while also publishing six books in a year.

If your family is supportive of your writing, ask them to help you find this time you need. This might mean getting your partner to watch the kids for an hour on a certain day, or setting aside funds to allow you to go out to a coffee shop to write once a week, or to rent a hotel room for a weekend to escape into your book.

WRITE IN SPRINTS

Now that you've found a few pockets of time to write, you should maximize what you're able to achieve in that time. Maybe you're thinking, "what's the point of having 20 minutes to write if all I do is stare at a blank screen?" The answer is – fill the screen with words.

Many writers find sprints effective to focus their writing time and fill the screen. To 'sprint' you set a timer for a short period of time. I find 20 minutes perfect for me, but you can experiment with anything from 10-30 minutes. As soon as you press GO, start writing. Don't stop. Don't think. Don't look at Facebook. Just write until the timer goes off. When it does, you're allowed a break for a couple of minutes. Get up. Jump around. Scroll your social media feeds. Then plonk your ass in the chair and start the timer again.

Up the ante by keeping a spreadsheet of your sprints. I write down the date and the number of words I've written for each sprint. I can see a visual record of a book's progress and whether I'm slacking off.

Before I started sprinting, I had no idea what my average word count per hour was. I suspect it was something like 500 words, possibly even less as I let social media and articles about writing distract me. Now I use sprinting, and I get between 400-700 words per sprint. I try to write 4k words per day – 2k in the morning, 2k in the afternoon. (Bear in mind I have no day job!) With sprinting I'm able to get my words done in a couple of hours, leaving me with more time in the day to work on my business (and watch cat videos on Youtube).

The reason sprinting works is because of brain chemistry. The timer tricks your brain into feeling a sense of urgency. When we have an endless amount of time stretching out before us, it's easy to get distracted and tell ourselves we have time to do things later.

Even though I got good grades during high school and college, I was a classic procrastinator. I'd stare at an empty screen for hours, trying to conjure an essay from thin air. As soon as my deadline approached and things got hairy, I'd be able to pull out something amazing. Using sprinting I'm able to recreate this productivity without actually butting up too close-for-comfort with my deadlines.

You can even sprint together with other writers and gamify your writing even more. Over in my Rage Against the Manuscript FB group, we use a tool called MyWriteClub to set up a sprinting 'room' and invite other writers to join the fun.

I've found sprinting really useful in my career, and perhaps you will, too.

FIND THE BEST TIME FOR YOU TO WRITE

There's a mantra you'll hear often: 'writers write every day.' It's... sometimes true, often not.

For many writers, myself included, writing every day is how we create good habits and improve our craft. For me, writing is a great joy and I look forward to sitting down to get my words out. Even when I had a day job, the time I carved out for my writing was often the highlight of my day.

But not all writers work like this. Some people find tying writing down into a specific time slot saps the joy from the creative process. I know several writers who produce 3-6 books per year while writing nothing for whole stretches of time, then locking themselves in a room or writers retreat and blasting through the entire book in a few days or weeks.

All that time when they're not writing, they're still working. They're percolating on the characters and story. They might jot notes down about scenes or plot twists. They're reading and researching. But the actual words come out in a giant burst of uninterrupted productivity.

In a similar way, some writers will do their best creative work early in the morning, before their household wakes up. Others like to wait for the dead of night, and others still are struck with late-afternoon inspiration. You need to try all different times to figure out when you're at your best.

I'm not going to tell you to 'write every day.' What I am going to say is that you should experiment with different techniques and times and methods and find out what works for you and what brings you the most joy.

KNOW WHAT YOU'RE GOING TO WRITE

Some people need to be prepared before they start writing. They need to know what happens and where the book is heading before they can put the words down. If you sit down and stare at a blank page, it's probably because you feel unprepared. You may be trying to do the hardest work (figuring out what happens next) in the most time-consuming way (while you're knee-deep in a scene). Working all the details out first *may* be the way you improve your speed. It certainly works for many writers.

However, you may be like me – you don't want an outline. I know a few basic things before I start writing. I have an idea of the protagonist's personality and desires. I have an overarching concept for the book and the world. I roughly know where I'm starting and how it's going to end, and I might have a couple of scenes in mind. I usually jot these things down and create an "outline" file – at this stage, it's about half a page of rough notes.

In order to write, I need to be in the character's head. If I create a detailed outline, I won't write the book. I know the story, so what's the point? It's not fun anymore. So I don't do it.

If this is you, there's a really great book I recommend you read. It's by an amazing historical fiction author named Libbie Hawker (she who writes in a number of different historical periods, mentioned in the pen names chapter) and it's called *Take Off Your Pants*. You'll also probably get a lot out of James Scott Bell's *Writing From the Middle*.

If you think you might be more of a plotter, I highly recommend several books. The Hero's Journey model designed by Joseph Campbell. Randy Ingermanson's Snowflake Method. Francesca Lia Block's part-memoir, part-writing-instructive, *The Thorn Necklace*. Jessica Brody's screen-writing technique *Save the Cat! Writes a Novel*. Lisa Cron's *Story Genius*. K. M. Weiland's *Structuring Your Novel*.

Most writers sit firmly in one camp or another. Try different outlining methods and see if it helps you. If it doesn't, don't force yourself to outline. Go with what works for *you*.

BEING KIND TO YOURSELF

You don't want to burn out on writing. Remember the core principle though which you should operate – it has to be fun. If you're not having fun and you're forcing yourself to write, that pain will be reflected in your words. If you're going through the motions, your readers will be able to tell, and you won't get any closer to your dreams.

Even though I've been super driven with my writing, 10+ years of working every spare moment when I wasn't at my day job have taken their toll from time to time. I thought I'd tell you a little cautionary tale about quitting my day job. OK, so I lied. It's not 'little.' Buckle up, cuz this is gonna take a while.

You already know that in Feb 2018 I got to do the super amazing incredible thing and quit my job as a copywriter at a tech startup to be a full-time author. What you might not know is that this isn't the first time I 'quit the day job' to be a writer. I did it in 2013. But less than six months later I was back in a salaried job.

I used to work as a braille transcriber. It was a wonderful job with great people that I enjoyed, but ever since I'd got out of university and realized I couldn't be an archaeologist, I'd been working toward this dream of writing full-time. I wanted to write novels and tell stories, but that was a long process involving submitting to editors and agents with no guarantees. I was young and impatient. I wanted it to happen NOW.

I think I've probably always been the type of person who really should be my own boss, and I was super keen to do that as soon as possible. I have been dreaming about quitting all my jobs basically ever since I started them. That's no reflection of the work I did, which was wonderful and rewarding, or the people I worked for, who were all lovely, but the fact that I kind of didn't want to work with people. I find all the 'office stuff' – meetings, commuting, small talk, team-building, filing, just urgh, *all of it* – distracted from work. I liked the people I worked with, but with only a couple of exceptions, they weren't my friends, and I found it hard to pretend otherwise.

I started spending a lot of time taking on freelance work for other small business owners because I liked their vibe and I thought if I could make enough money doing that, I'd be able to buy myself more time to write fiction. I would get home from my day job and work until bedtime on client websites or tinkering with my novels.

After a few years, I had more freelance work than hours in the day. I was getting seriously burned out working all the time. I was pulling in enough money for the hours I was putting in that my husband and I decided we'd take the chance and I'd quit my job and write full time. At first, I stepped down to three days a week at my day job, then I built up the courage (and that was a lot of building) to go fully freelance.

I could work from home! I could set my own hours and be my own boss! I could have more free time for writing fiction! I was living the dream!

Hahahaha.

Turns out, I hated it. I was MISERABLE.

I worked more than ever. I could never switch off. I felt this incredible pressure to earn a certain amount of money to prove I could do it (this didn't come from my husband or other people – it came from me). I felt like if I wasn't working then I was wasting time.

I hadn't got used to the idea that a business owner's to-do list ever ends. I'd keep thinking, "I'll write these three articles and then I'll work on my book." But after those three articles there would always be three more, and three more after that. I felt trapped. The timing was bad because we'd started to build our dream home. Money was tight, and I felt that if the whole thing fell apart it would be my fault.

I resented working to help other people achieve their creative dreams while mine sat on the backburner. I resented clients who argued, who refused to pay their invoices, who wanted more more more for less money (and I was already way undercharging, which was also another issue).

I had no time for my own fiction because this pressure I put on myself to get client work done was too great. When I *did* sit down to write fiction, the words wouldn't come. I didn't have anything left for myself.

I cried because an editor I'd been working with for years left and a deal that would see my books published fell through. I cried because it felt like all my hard work was for nothing.

I hated it so much that after six months, when one of my clients begged me to take a full-time job as a copywriter, offering me over 50% more than what I had earned at my last position as a starting salary and said I could work three days a week from home, I took the job happily.

I felt like a failure. But I was determined that I'd learn from my mistakes. I wasn't going to repeat this.

I quit every one of my freelance clients. I accepted that running a service business wasn't where my passion or skills lie.

I declared that when my work hours were done, I would STOP WORKING. I was a good worker for the 40 hours I was at the job, but I never put in unpaid overtime even though it might have cost me some promotions. I was done giving all my creative energy to other people. I loved the 'think fast and break things' mentality of tech and the idea that shipping product is better than waiting until it's 100% perfect (I've probably carried a lot of that over into my own business), but I didn't love the mentality that the company was your life. I didn't want to use all my creative energy making someone else rich.

(Also, there are only so many ways to make accounting software and vinyl siding interesting. OK, not many ways at all).

I spent my free time working on my books. I learned

about self-publishing. I dedicated myself to being a successful indie, but ONLY if I was having fun doing it.

I decided that I didn't have the fortitude to start a business and build a house at the same time. So I set myself a rule that I'd wait until the house was finished before I considered quitting again.

I taught myself to be grateful to my day job for giving me the money to pay the mortgage while I learned and grew my readership and dealt with the stress of building.

I (tried to) stopped beating myself up and calling myself a failure, because it wasn't true.

I (tried to) have better balance in my life. It worked. For a while. And then the old burnout crept back.

I was able to work from home three days a week at my first two positions, but because I'm blind and can't drive myself, my commute was 1:45 each way at one job and 1:30 each way at the next. I had to leave at a certain time to get a bus to my husband's office so we could drive home together. Sometimes when you are disabled riding public transport can be stressful – people can be rude and things go wrong and you don't know what's happened. It seemed dumb to do that stress and commuting just to sit in the office with my headphones jammed in my ears because everyone talking around me was a distraction.

In 2017 I was at a marketing agency, and the company basically imploded. They lost their breadwinner client, and I came to work one day and discovered our team of eight was now a team of three. My husband and I were halfway through building a house. I'd just released a book that was a complete flop. I felt afraid for my financial security.

My husband thought it was the ideal time to quit, but I worried things would end up like last time. I also felt like staying at the agency was a bad idea. I was stressing about it. I hated the work. I hated the not-knowing. So I decided to leave. Maybe I'd look for something else. Maybe I'd write. I wasn't 100% sure.

The week I handed in my notice, my old boss from my first tech job called me. "Are you happy where you are?" he asked. "Because I've just become the marketing manager at a startup, and I have to build a team..."

I liked this guy. He was hard work, but I knew how to handle him. He challenged me constantly and understood my work-from-home needs and introvert ways, which I appreciated. I went to talk to the company CEO, and we got along well. I asked for an insane amount of money and they said yes.

There was a catch. Part of the culture of the company wanted everyone in the office, eating lunch together, brainstorming, etc. They wanted me to come in every day. I said two days. They said four days. It was 1:45 mins each way from my house.

My husband and I discussed it. We knew the next year was going to be what we needed to finish the house. We knew this job would mean a lot of extra work for me. It would be stressful, but I'd done stressful before and survived. "It's your call," he said. "But I think if you do it, you should put an end date on it. In a year, you leave and you write full-time."

So I said yes. And there began the most stressful year of my life.

The day before I started at work, my boss emailed me: "Oh, by the way, our office moved to a new suburb. Hope that's okay." The new suburb meant my commute now included a car ride and TWO buses and was 2:30 each way – 5 hours round-trip commuting and I had to leave work early to get to my husband, so I'd have to make up time when I got home.

I went in four days a week and had a bit of a meltdown after a month where I cried in a meeting because I was so tired and my back hurt (I was working hunched over a computer on the bus and in the car so I didn't have to work when I got home). Begrudgingly, they allowed me to drop down to three days a week in the office.

I wrote my quitting date in my calendar.

I did the math on the minimum I had to earn each month so we could pay the mortgage and keep our cats fed. I was about halfway to that number with my fiction. I knew I'd have to either have a hit book OR make up the rest with free-lance work.

I didn't want to count on a hit, so I put up a Facebook status saying I was looking for freelance work. I knew what I wanted – to work through an agency. They'd handle the clients, I'd just write things, which was the easy part for me. I ended up with work through a friend's brother, and he referred me to another agency, and before I knew it I had four small marketing studios giving me work. I was prepping to quit. The only thing was, it was only March/April – the house *still* wasn't finished, and I had to do this freelance work alongside my demanding copy job. AND writing my own books.

Here we go again.

I worked non-stop, basically from the moment I got up until I went to bed. I had my computer in front of me every night while we watched TV. I gave up weekend plans to work. I was basically doing two full-time jobs.

We poured the extra money into finishing the house and building some savings. We were getting closer to our goal, to the life we wanted.

This year strained my marriage like nothing else. We were stressed about the house. Even in the moments when my husband and I hung out, I wasn't really present. I accepted too many invitations to go away to hike, to see friends, to teach writing and officiate weddings for extra money, just to get away from my computer. He felt as though I was getting away from him.

But... we had that end-date. Gods, how I looked to that end-date with so much hope.

I didn't have a hit that year. In fact, my writing income dipped for the first six months. My dream looked further away than ever. But then I had my first BookBub (more on this later), and things picked up.

I had so little time to work on my fiction that I focused only on the thing that made the most money – I wrote books. I didn't update Facebook or my blog or do pretty much any marketing apart from applying for BookBubs and sending out a newsletter when I published.

By the time November rolled around, I'd put on weight and I felt on the verge of crying ALL THE TIME. My brain turned to mush and the whole world felt sort of far away, like I was listening through water. I knew I was probably close to having a breakdown. I felt like I couldn't talk to people about it, because I had done this to myself. Anyone I talked to would have (rightfully so) said, "So just stop."

December rolled around, and I was so close, so close. I started reading reverse harem books. An idea came to me. I wrote *The Castle of Earth and Embers* in a flurry of inspiration – churning out 2,000 words a day on my bus commute with my laptop balanced precariously on my knees.

The excitement over that book was probably what got me through those last couple of months.

I released it the same day I handed in my notice, and it instantly became my bestselling book of all time. For the first month ever I hit my income goal solely from fiction. It felt like a fucking sign from the universe.

One year nearly to the day since I started at that job, I said goodbye to the 5-hour commute. I had my last doughnut morning tea with my workmates. I went home in a daze. I couldn't quite believe it.

On my first day as a full-time writer, I bounced out of bed at the crack of dawn. I wrote 5k words on *The Castle of Fire and Fable*. I cooked dinner and played with the cats. I ACTU-ALLY watched a movie with my husband. It was the best day in a very long time.

I spent 2018 writing the Briarwood series and focusing on growing my fiction income. I increased my financial goal, and one by one I dropped the agencies as clients as I got closer to that goal. I started to put long-term plans into action to ensure the business was sustainable.

I (mostly) stopped working in the evenings and weekends. The house was basically done. My husband and I worked hard to communicate better and to enjoy the house and life we'd built. It was one of the BEST years of our marriage.

So that's my 'how I quit' story. It's also my 'do as I say, not as I do' story about being kind to yourself and not giving yourself a breakdown over writing, cuz it's not worth it. *(Except when it is)*.

Probably don't do what I did and work yourself toward burnout and hurt your marriage. But having the 'end-date' thing was a great idea, as was using more stable freelance work as a transition. Also, stash some money in the bank. We had a few months of mortgage payments as a buffer. Quitting wasn't a financial decision so much as a mental health one for me. I needed to make this happen. I needed to know if I could do it. And that was the best decision I ever made.

What I've tried to show you in this section is how you might be able to increase your output. You're going to have to do some experimenting and figure out what works for you. Gamifying your process with sprints might be awesome for you, or it might make you feel trapped. Getting away for a few days might help you smash out an entire novel, or you could spend the whole time staring blankly at the wall. Plotting out your book in detail with index cards and spreadsheets might help you get to grips with the story, or it could make you feel as though the whole exercise is pointless. We're all different and our brains respond in unique ways.

To me, it all comes back to my mantra of having fun. If a technique feels too much like hard work, like you're trying to stifle your creativity, ditch it. Find what feels fun and effortless to you, and just do more of that.

Becca Syme is a lovely person and an author who has developed solid techniques for writing faster. Listen to an awesome interview she did on the SPA Girls podcast.

Rachel Aaron is another author who writes a lot about hacking her process. She went from writing 2k a day to 10k a day, and she's got an amazing book called – not surprisingly – *2k to 10k – Writing Faster, Writing Better, and Writing More of What You Love* – all about her process.

YOU ARE YOUR OWN PUBLISHING HOUSE

When you're writing and editing your book, you are a creative. You get to live inside your characters and do all the artsy thinking that makes writing so much fun.

However, at all other times, you need to put aside your writer brain and engage your publisher brain. I've already introduced you to my 'hat' analogy. Imagine yourself putting down your writer hat as soon as you write 'THE END' and picking up your publisher hat.

A publisher can still be creative, but they're also an astute business person. They know the market, they've done their research, and they can make strategic decisions that will drive their company forward.

For example, you-the-writer may have five different ideas for what you want to write next. That's the creative part.

You-the-publisher will have to look at those ideas strategically and think about what's the best fit for your current backlist and what is likely to get you closer to your goals.

(If you-the-publisher is particularly savvy, you might be checking out the bestseller charts in your genre, looking at trends and covers, and thinking about how you could work your ideas to fit one of those trends).

You-the-publisher gets the fun job of planning your releases for any given year. Because you've only got one writer (you!) and finite resources, you'll only have so many release spots to fill. You have to think carefully about how best to use those spots.

After you-the-publisher has done your thing, you-the-marketer has the job of making sure as many readers as possible are aware of the books you release.

Switching between your three hats is a concept I will refer back to, because I think it helps you to compartmentalize. If you've never run a business before, you will need to learn some new skills. That's cool – learning is interesting. And maybe you think that you won't be good at business, but a) I bet that's not true and b) remember that all sorts of people run successful businesses in vastly different ways. Just like there are no real rules in writing, there's no 'one rule of business,' and you get to decide what works for you.

As the publishing house, you get to decide the rules and set the release schedule. You can change things if they aren't working. You can crack the whip when you need to and give yourself a fucking break when things feel overwhelming. You're the boss, so be the kind of boss you've always wanted – fun, clever, and kind.

HOW TO ROCK WRITING FASTER:

- How fast do you write right now? Can you get some sense of the number of words you write in a day? This will give you a starting point.
- Put on your publishing hat and look strategically at your publishing schedule. Choose projects that are most likely to bring you closer to your goals. Set a schedule that's workable but just a *little* beyond your reach. If it's taken you a year to write your first book, you probably can't go straight into writing a book a month, but can you produce two books this year? What about three? Four can't be that hard...
- Find a space to carve out 20 minutes per day to write. Enlist your family or roommates to help you keep on track.
- Sprint. Set the timer and go, go, go!
- If sprinting isn't for you, try binge-writing. Schedule a few days where you have no interruptions. Get out of the house if possible. Send the kids to their grandparents'. Go, go, go!
- Try writing at different times of the day. Notice when writing feels joyful and flows freely. Notice when you struggle for every word.
- Read writing craft/outline books and try different techniques. Throw away what feels like work and keep anything that makes writing more fun.
- Track your progress in a notebook or spreadsheet. For each sprint, write down the number of words you write and a total for the day. Let your growing word count be a motivation!
- Get some writer accountability buddies. You might

find a fellow writer on Rage Against The Manuscript to sprint with and share your triumphs!

- Be aware of the signs of burnout and fatigue. Make sure you have people in your life who will call you on your bullshit when you need them – because if you're anything like me, you'll forget to take care of yourself sometimes.

Chapter Eight

STEP 5. MAKE READING ENJOYABLE

If you want to keep readers coming back for more of your books, you need to give them a good reading experience. This means not springing nasty surprises on them that are outside their genre – for example, killing off the hero in a romance novel, or suddenly turning a cozy mystery into a horror story. It also means crafting the best story possible – free of typos and continuity or grammatical errors.

As the author, you can improve the enjoyment of your readers by:

1. Writing 'to market' and following genre conventions.
2. Using an editor/proofreader.
3. Using formatting to create an easy reading experience.
4. Only put out your best work.

Let's look at these one at a time.

WRITING WHAT YOUR READERS WANT

Being a writer means pouring your heart onto the page. But it also means acknowledging that writing involves two parties – the writer and the audience. The people who make a living writing or see success with their projects consider their audience at least as much as they consider their own proclivities.

If you want readers to keep buying your books, you've got to give them what they want. What readers want is, "More of the same stuff I love with some fun twists."

We've talked a little about genre in previous chapters, especially about how genre informs the way readers search for books. Within each genre, there are certain unwritten 'rules.' Sometimes writers break those rules and are very successful, but those are usually writers who already have a big audience and who are strategically moving outside of conventions. They are the exceptions – I choose to believe I'm not going to be the exception.

Generally speaking, you need to follow the rules of your genre if you want to appeal to readers. Give them more of the same stories they love, just with a fresh twist.

In a detective story, the mystery is always unraveled at the end of the book. In a romance, the couple overcomes their obstacles and get their happily-ever-after. In fantasy, good triumphs over evil. You should know the tropes and features of your genre because you should be reading in the genre you write in. TV Tropes (www.tvtropes.org) is also a great site to look at for lists of common tropes, as is just searching online for common tropes in your genre. (Warning: TV Tropes is a rabbit hole of fascination and you will be lost for days).

We call this 'writing to market.' Authors will often talk about 'writing to trend' and 'writing to market.' These two things are common techniques authors use to find and grow their audience. They may sound like synonyms, but they refer to specific techniques:

WRITING TO TREND

This means spotting trends before they hit it big and being one of the earliest authors out with a trendy book. Trends swing in and out of favor with readers – what's hot one month may be gone the next. Many traditional publishers try to predict trends, but it's hard for them because they schedule books a year (or more) before they're published. As a self-published author, you can have a book to market in a month or less, so you can jump on an emerging trend.

You have to be fast to spot a trend before it gets big and get your book out, because there are lots of authors (many with huge followings) doing the same thing. If you're too late on a trend, your book will be crushed by the competition.

There's a lot of potential money to be made if you get in early on a trend, but long-term it can hurt your business. If you're always jumping on the next-big-thing, you may not be building a cohesive author brand. You may also be stressing yourself out and relying on big hits.

The romance genre (where I write) has seen its share of trends over the years. A few years ago, it was stepbrother romances. Right now it is bully romance. Paranormal has historically been all about vampires, but for the last decade, it's been all-shifters-all-the-time. Now Academy books styled after Harry Potter are the big thing. What's next? Who knows?

WRITING TO MARKET

Writing to market means that instead of going off on what-ever weird thing YOU want to write, you create the types of stories your readers have already told you (with their buying habits) that they love. A to-market book may also be trendy, but they tend to be more evergreen because they focus on tried-and-true favorite reader tropes.

This doesn't mean you're 'selling out.' Don't let anyone tell you that! If you genuinely love your genre and your work, then there is nothing wrong with being smart about what you choose to write for whom. This is you wearing your publishing hat and using the information available to make the best business decisions.

Remember what I said right from the start? If you're not having fun in this business, then what are you doing here? There are much easier ways to make a living. But you can have a total blast writing to market. In fact, I think it's more fun because you end up with a bigger audience – and readers are seriously the coolest people. I want to hang out with them all the time.

Both writing to market and writing trends involves studying your genre and its readers. You've got to get to know them like they were your BFFs. Figure out what resonates in the stories they love, and give them more of THAT. It means keeping a close eye on the bestseller lists in your genre and which books readers are talking about. It means reading widely in your genre and identifying what works and doesn't work *for readers*. It means analyzing covers and blurbs and characters and collecting data to improve your craft and marketing.

The only difference between writing to market and writing trends is that trends take the lessons learned from writing to market and apply them to tropes and niches and subgenres that readers are gagging for RIGHT NOW. That trend may wane weeks or months from now, so they need to get on it while it's hot.

If you're writing to market, you may find that sometimes

you are perfectly positioned to spot and react to trends. This happened to me with my Kings of Miskatonic Prep series. Because I was paying careful attention to the market and I'd worked hard to hone my process where I could write fast, I was able to come up with an idea I knew my readers would love that spoke to an emerging trend, get the pre-order up ASAP, write the book in three weeks, and be one of the early books. It was an amazing stroke of luck that propelled that series to the top of the Amazon charts, but I don't count on that kind of success with every release. I won't be 'on trend' every time, but I will always be giving my readers what they crave.

If you want to learn more about writing to market, check out *Write to Market* by Chris Fox.

BETA-READERS, EDITORS, AND PROOFREADERS

Have at least one person *who is not you* read over your work. Ideally, you should hire a professional editor and/or proofreader to ensure you're giving readers a quality book. Some editors and proofreaders specialize in working with indies, and they are affordable. I pay around $300 for my editor and $100 for my proofreader.

If that's too much for you right now, you may be able to swap services with another author or editor, or bribe a friend or family member who's great at grammar to take a look. Even using free programs like Grammarly (www.grammarly.com) or having your computer read your manuscript aloud will help you spot mistakes and clunky sentences.

There are lots of different types of useful people writers use. You'll see other writers talking about their:

- **Beta-reader:** Someone who casts a critical eye over your manuscript before it goes to any other editor. Usually, betas aren't professional editors, but they are voracious readers. Instead of picking up typos, they focus on story stuff – are they excited during this chapter? Does the protagonist resonate? Is someone acting out of character? Do they notice continuity or plot errors?

Incorporating their feedback can help make your story more engaging and fix wider issues. Many of my friends send their betas each chapter as they complete it. This freaks me out! I have one beta – my husband – and I give him the manuscript as soon as I've finished. He has two weeks to give me feedback.

- **Developmental editor:** Kind of a professional version of a beta-reader. Your developmental editor will give you feedback on your style, plot, characters, and the big picture of your book.
- **Editor/line editor/copy editor:** Different people call this stage different things. I just call it 'editing,' and I work with a professional who goes over my manuscript like a boss. She picks up spelling and grammar my Grammarly pass missed, but also style issues like repetitive prose and continuity, and offers suggestions to improve tension or syntax, word choice, and strength of prose.
- **Proofreader:** A final pass to pick up stray typos and grammar issues. Your proofreader is the last person to see the manuscript.

There's no law that says you need all four of them, or any of them. It's up to you to find a process that works for you. Personally, I put my manuscript through Grammarly to catch most glaring errors, then I use a beta-reader (the aforementioned cantankerous drummer husband) and a professional editor. Sometimes a proofreader, but I've found this less essential as I've improved my craft and process.

Even with professional editors, mistakes creep through or you introduce your own errors. On my July 2017 release, I had a minor character named Rita. My editor suggested her name was too close to my main character's name, Rosa. I went to my manuscript and did a find/replace all on Rita's name with a substitute – Margaret. Problem solved. I launched the book. It sold around 3,500 copies before a reader emailed me to tell me that three times in the book I had the word hemargaretge, and was this possibly a spelling error? It turns out that when I did that find/replace I'd also changed the word 'heritage' to 'hemargaretge' and NO ONE had pointed it out.

Once I stopped feeling sick, I was able to laugh about it.

The point of that story is to remind you to be VERY careful with find/replace, especially on your final manuscript. But also, to tell you that readers don't need your book to be *perfect*. They want a good story. If you have too many errors it will impact their ability to read, and that will annoy them – and they'll tell you in reviews. However, if you tell a good yarn and you've got a few spelling mistakes, they'll still consider you a favorite author.

I try to always think of my writing as a business (because it is). Don't bring an inferior product to market. Get the best editing and cover you can within your budget. Find a process that works for you. But don't spend years fiddling and proofing the book as an excuse to not publish it – no matter how many times you read through, you'll still miss mistakes and you'll still want to tweak the prose. At some point, you've got to take the plunge and hit publish.

FORMATTING

Formatting your work for publishing means creating a lovely document that your reader's device can understand. Their device will then present your work in the best possible way and enable them to view images, click on links, see bold and italics, and use a table of contents to jump around the book.

First I'm going to talk about ebook formatting. The reason for this is that if you whip your file into shape for an ebook, you can use that same file to create a paperback in less time, but it will be a bit harder the other way around. Your formatted file will also be useful to give to your audiobook narrator.

The word processing program you use to write your work will give you a certain file type – usually a doc, docx, or txt. This file may look nice and tidy to you on your computer screen, but what really matters is the code going on in the background. When the file is converted to the ereader format (MOBI or EPUB), the computer has to be given the correct signals so it knows when a chapter begins, when a word is bolded, and when there's a link in the text.

You can upload a docx file as is to Amazon and it will create an ebook. However, that ebook won't be a joy to read. People won't be able to navigate through the chapters. It might have random sections in a different font. Tables and bulleted lists will probably be a total mess. This is because what you see on your screen isn't the same as what appears on an ereader. The words will be the same, but if you haven't used the right formatting language, the ereader won't know where a chapter begins or why a text has five hard returns.

You want readers to be able to navigate the file – skip to a chapter they want to read, see headings and subheadings, notice quotations by indenting them, etc. Putting in these features during the word processing stage has to be done in a certain way if you want them to carry through the conversion process.

A properly formatting file is also a huge benefit to anyone with a print disability (for example, visually-impaired or blind readers like me) as it will enable their screen reader to pick up on formatting.

HOW TO FORMAT YOUR EBOOK FILE

Start with a file that's as 'clean' as possible. If you use 'styles' in MS Word, Google Docs, etc, then you'll be ensuring your file is free from strange formatting that will cause problems during conversion. You'll also be creating a file that can be navigated.

The first thing you do before you try any formatting is to select all the text in your file and click 'normal style.' This will delete any back-end code you've accidentally added during the writing process, and gives you that 'clean' file while retaining style elements like italics. Now, go through the file and add headings, bulleted lists using styles, links, and page breaks (never hit the 'return' key multiple times to break a page – always use 'insert > page break').

Using styles means that if you have a chapter heading 'chapter 1', instead of highlighting those words and choosing a font and a text size and centering them on the page, you highlight and select 'heading 1' from the styles/formatting dropdown menu. Use 'heading 1' for all chapter headings, 'heading 2' for all subheadings, and 'blockquotes' for any quoted text.

You can now create a table of contents by writing out a list of chapter headings and then linking each one within your file to the corresponding chapter heading. Add front matter (copyright page, an epigraph, dedication) and back matter (about the author, other books by the author, excerpt or blurb for a future book in the series, link to sign up to your newsletter, etc) separating each element with a page break.

This is how you manually format a file. Most authors don't do this – it will generate a perfectly readable but generic-looking ebook file, and it will take you time to learn and perfect.

I use Vellum (www.vellum.pub), which is software I've licensed that will create beautiful ebooks and print books in no time at all. Vellum has been hands down one of the best investments I've ever made in my business. Currently, Vellum is Mac-only, but many PC users run it by using a service called MacinCloud.

There are other ways to get your formatting done. Many people use a program called Calibre. The Draft2Digital distributor offers a free formatting tool for ebook and print, and Amazon has Kindle Create, which is a free Kindle-only formatting tool.

You could also outsource your formatting to another company. If you're only writing a single book or you find the concepts above a real headache, then this might be a good option for you. Personally, I feel that formatting is so easy to learn I'd look at doing it yourself to save on production costs if at all possible. Doing it yourself means you can quickly make changes to an ebook or print file without having to pay extra or wait in a work queue.

Note on images: Kindle adds a 'delivery fee' to cover the cost of sending your file to a Kindle. The larger your formatted file, the higher this delivery fee. If you use tons of large images, your delivery fee might get so high it eats significantly into your royalty. If possible, cut back images in the ebook to only the essentials, or use the Kindle Kids' Book Creator, Kindle Comic Creator, or Kindle Textbook Creator, which are all specifically designed for books with tons of images.

You might like to cut some images and include them instead as bonus content for a newsletter signup or on your website, or save them for social media sharing.

Once you have this clean file for your ebook, you can import it into a print template to create your print formatting. Both KDP Print and IngramSpark offer print templates in a variety of sizes, which will help you make sense of common print issues like widow/orphans and page numbering. Or, like me, you could use Vellum. Sweet, sweet headache-saving Vellum.

PRODUCING YOUR BEST WORK

My last point, and I think this goes without saying for you, but I'm gonna say it anyway, is not to just churn out any old guff because you think it will sell. Respect your readers. Give them a book you care about, and they'll care about it, too.

PIRACY AND DRM

Any time I run a publishing class, I'm asked about DRM and about how to stop people from pirating my book. My answer is, "I don't."

Why? The majority of readers are wonderful people who are perfectly happy to pay for a book to be sent directly to their device. Those are the readers I write for, and I want to make it as easy as possible for them to enjoy my books across all their devices. DRM makes it harder for them to access my books, and it makes life especially difficult for blind and low-vision readers (of which I am one).

Piracy will happen whatever I do. If I scour the internet for illegal downloads of my books and send DMCA takedown notices, the books will be back up in a few days. If I use DRM on my books, a skilled pirate can break it in minutes. I choose to accept that piracy comes hand-in-hand with building an audience, and so I let it go on as long as it doesn't impact my career.

When piracy becomes an issue is when it does affect your career. I've heard of authors who have run afoul of Amazon's algorithms because pirated books are technically breaking KU's exclusivity clauses. Usually, showing Amazon that you've sent a takedown notice and that those books are up on known pirate sites will get them off your back, but as you may come to discover, dealing with Amazon will yield different results depending on who you talk to, the day of the week, the phase of the moon, and how many goats you sacrifice.

(No goats were harmed in the publishing of this book).

HOW TO MAKE YOUR BOOKS A JOY TO READ:

- Figure out what budget you have available for producing your book. For your first book, you have four main potential costs: cover, editing, formatting, and marketing. If you need to prioritize where to spend money, make cover/editing number one.
- Study your market/genre/niche. You might like to create spreadsheets and list titles with your observations, or you could just look through the bestseller lists and take note of what you see. You should be reading books in your genre so you know what readers are craving.
- Figure out five things readers crave that you can include in your novel – tropes, character types, cover elements, etc. Are you hitting the beats that make readers come back for more?
- Look for beta-readers or an editor. Ask around in

your friend/family circles, or talk to other writers for their recommendations. Most service providers will edit a few pages for free as a sample. It may take you a few tries to find someone you really click with, but once you do it'll be like finding the perfect hairdresser – you'll never let them go.

- Be open to criticism. This is harder than it sounds, and it may take you time to work through the resistance of hearing people critique your work. Difficult, but essential to improving as a writer. Remember, if you surround yourself with the right people, they are never critiquing you as a person, only what you've created, and only because they want to help you make it the best it can be.

- Try formatting your ebook file from scratch, just to see how you do. The more you can use styles and clean formatting, the better you'll find your formatting experience whether you DIY or use a tool like Vellum. You'll find plenty of follow-along tutorials on YouTube if you're feeling confused.

- Ask yourself, "Am I proud of this book?" and "Am I having fun?" If the answer is yes, then it doesn't matter what happens when you publish or what other people say about you, you've done an awesome thing!

Chapter Nine

STEP 6. COVER. TITLE. BLURB: THEY MATTER

As an indie author without direct distribution into book-stores, you're probably going to make most of your sales online as digital ebooks.

As you learned in the first chapter, research from Author Earnings has shown 65% of readers now prefer digital devices for fiction. Other markets (non-fiction, children's books, etc) are growing, too. Certain genres will always have a huge print market – coffee table books, children's picture books, literary fiction, etc – and it's important as an author and publisher to understand how people in your genre are reading your books. It will likely be digitally.

Even if you're not a digital reader yourself, you need to find ways to reach those readers. And that means under-standing how they search for and choose books.

YOUR TITLE

For most of us, the title of your book will appear during the writing process. I usually have my title in place before I even start writing. For fiction, your title should speak to the genre you're writing and evoke something of the mood, setting, and character of the book. Fun books might employ puns and other word tricks to alert readers to the character voice. Darker books will use emotive language to evoke mood and setting. Objects and names can be used to create a certain look and feel. If you have a unique plot element, character trait, or setting, you might like to pick out this fact using the title.

Look at how other authors in your genre title their work. Without copying, can you use the same patterns and language to convey to readers they might enjoy your book? Experiment with different words and lengths until you come up with something you like. If you can't choose between different titles, test them out on readers or fellow writers you trust.

For non-fiction, your title needs to clearly state the purpose of the book and what the reader will learn. It's also great if it can convey something of the book's style and tone so the reader knows what type of experience they can expect. For example, this book – How to Rock Self-Publishing – tells you exactly what you're going to learn about (self-publishing) while also letting you know it's gonna be served up with a bit of my punk/metal ethos.

You also want your non-fiction title to elicit an emotional response. Your readers have a specific problem – they pick up your book because they believe you have a solution. Beware of a title that repeats their problem back to them. This will give an emotional response, all right – one of fear and resentment. Instead, focus on how your book will solve the problem for them, and how they will learn new skills to reach their desired end-state.

For individual titles in a series, consider following a pattern. All my series have a distinct pattern that makes it clear the books belong together. For example, my Briarwood Witches series has five books as follows:

- The Castle of Earth and Embers
- The Castle of Fire and Fable
- The Castle of Water and Woe
- The Castle of Wind and Whispers
- The Castle of Spirit and Sorrow

I did a similar thing for my Wolves of Crookshollow series:

- Digging the Wolf
- Writing the Wolf
- Inking the Wolf
- Wedding the Wolf

And my Kings of Miskatonic Prep series all have one-word titles in the past tense:

- Shunned
- Initiated
- Possessed
- Ignited

You might like to enlist your readers to help you come up with titles, especially for future books in a series. My Nevermore Bookshop Mysteries series titles all include murderous puns of famous book titles or bookish phrases. I had a few ideas in place for the series when I enlisted the help of my readers. They came up with some AMAZING ideas. I have six titles in the series, and about four more amazing titles saved up in case I get the chance to write more in the future.

If you're writing a series, you'll also need a series title.

Again, look for themes and elements important to the story that stretch across all four books. Most importantly, your series title should convey your genre. You can be overt about this and use keywords in your series title. For example, cozy mystery writer H. Y. Hanna has the Bewitched by Chocolate Mysteries (paranormal witchy mystery series set in a chocolate shop) and the English Cottage Garden Mysteries (murder mysteries focused around an English cottage garden/nursery). Fans of the genre can tell just from the series title if the books involve elements they enjoy.

Speak your title aloud. Does it roll off your tongue? Is it easy to remember and repeat? You want people to recall your title so they can tell their friends all about it.

Once you've come up with a book/series title, it's probably worthwhile searching it on Amazon to see what other books have been published with the same title. You can still use a title if another author has used it (unless it's trademarked), but you don't want readers to get confused, so I'd avoid this if the other title is a similar genre.

YOUR BOOK COVER

People browsing online first see your book's cover in thumbnail form, so it needs to be bold and eye-catching. Your cover needs to look similar to other covers in your genre (so readers can find what they want to read) but also stand out because of its beautiful design and bold title. This sounds hard to achieve, and it is. That's why it's best to hire a specialist book cover designer to create an amazing cover for you. There are plenty of designers who specialize in book covers for indie authors, and they're relatively affordable. I pay between $150–500 for my book covers.

If that's unaffordable for you right now, consider a premade cover. Many cover designers will offer a selection of 'premade' or template cover designs for $30-70. You choose one that suits your book and genre, and the designer will exchange the placeholder text with your author name and book title. You won't be able to make other changes to the cover, but you'll have a professional design ready to rock. You could always upgrade your books with new covers later if they do well.

Remember how we spoke about your author branding? This should be present on your covers. A reader should be able to look at one of your books and instantly recognize it as yours. Most authors do this by keeping the same font and placement for their name, and by ensuring their name is large and bold so it can be seen in thumbnail.

Series branding is also important. Books in the same series should retain a similar look/feel/color scheme/font throughout. When you hire your cover designer, make sure they know how many books are in the series so they can choose a cover model with multiple poses. Look for premade series book covers – if you find a cover you like but it's only a single, ask the designer if they'd be able to create it into a series.

OTHER TIPS FOR BOOK COVERS

Think like a reader. As a writer, you may be tempted to choose the most unusual and visually impactful design. If it doesn't look like other books in the genre then readers won't be able to identify your book as something they'd enjoy.

Likewise, leave behind fancy scrollwork lettering and tiny fonts – your title and name need to be big and bold so they can be read in thumbnail size.

Stay on top of genre trends. If you use cover elements that were big 10-20 years ago, you risk having your books look old and tired. Browse the top 100 book lists in your genres on Amazon and the other platforms to see what's selling in your genre *now*.

Some authors like to hang out in cover designer groups and use the premade covers designers put up as research into what authors are writing now for release in 2-3 months. This sounds like a great idea in theory, but be wary. A couple of years back we saw *mermaidpalooza* – every paranormal and fantasy cover designer was making mermaid book covers. Many predicted mermaid was a growing trend, but this wasn't reflected in the bestseller lists or in the number of mermaid books hitting the shelves.

Give good instructions to your designer. Your designer can only go off the information you provide them. Every designer I've used has a questionnaire I fill in for each book/series, outlining what the book is about and the mood/feeling I want for the cover.

Pick out key elements of the story the designer can high-light on the cover – for example, for my Kings of Miskatonic Prep series, I gave my designer a list of objects that had some symbolic meaning in the series: theatre mask, book, tiara, skull, candle, artist palette, occult items, knife, diploma, etc. She chose some of these elements to use as the focal point on the covers.

If you need models on the cover, provide details like hair and eye color, and the amount of flexibility you have with these. It's really helpful to provide examples of other covers in your genre you like. It's even more useful to explain in a sentence or two what you like/don't like about those covers.

Use your fans. If you have a decent-sized fanbase, you might like to add a poll or simply ask for opinions about different cover options. Make sure to ask the designer for permission first – some don't like to have draft projects avail-able for public viewing.

Do a cover reveal. A great piece of social media content is to reveal your cover to your readers in a post. This helps get them excited about the book before it's even live.

YOUR BOOK BLURB

Once the reader clicks on your book cover, they're taken to a product page where your blurb has to entice them to read the book. Writing blurbs isn't easy (I find them harder than writing the actual book!) but it's an essential skill to master if you want to sell books.

Your blurb is a short (150-250 words) description of your book for the purpose of enticing readers to hit BUY, or at least open the cover and take a look inside. Your blurb isn't a summary of the book – no, no, no, no. Instead, it gives the reader a sense of the main character, their key problem, the big bad looming danger on the horizon, and the genre of the book (aka, whether they can expect dragons or not. No surprise dragons. If there are dragons in your book, they should be on the cover, cuz dragons sell books. If there are no dragons, don't mention the dragons. You have been warned).

For non-fiction, your blurb will allow the reader to identify with the problem they're having and see a way forward toward solving it. You need to give them confidence you can solve it (often by explaining your credentials) and show them what they can expect on the other side.

I like to begin my blurb with a short, snappy one-sentence hook. Amazon will show this on its product search pages, so it's a great way to hook readers. I'll often use short phrases to list things that readers will encounter in the book. Lists of three or five problems are common in blurbs.

Blurbs are traditionally strictly in third-person, but I write mine mostly in first person. I like throwing the reader right into that character's voice. Your blurb is all about character – don't pack it full of plot elements. Instead, focus on helping readers to get to know your protagonist and what messy jam they're going to get involved in.

Keep your blurb action-packed and full of conflict. You'll probably be focusing mainly on external conflict and consequences. The reader needs to sense the danger and understand why the danger is, well... dangerous. For certain genres in particular (romance, I'm looking at you), you might want to include a bit of that juicy internal conflict, as well.

Don't be afraid to mess with the format of blurbs. Use single word paragraphs for impact. Write the blurb in text-speak, if that relates to the book. Write a laundry list – my friend KT Strange did this in her bestselling book *Phoenixcry*. That is blurb perfection.

Include the common tropes of your genre to alert readers that they'll love your story. Tropes are reader shorthand for 'story crack' – aka, addictive books they can't put down. You can do this overtly, by actually listing tropes in your blurb. Romance books often do this, stating the book is a 'friends-to-lovers romance' or a 'secret-baby romance.' You should know the common tropes in your genre from reading widely within it. Look at sites like TV Tropes for ideas.

Another way authors signal to readers that they'll love a book is to compare it to other known titles/pop culture references. Do this sparingly and carefully – make sure the comparison is a fair one, or readers won't trust you in the future. For example, in my Nevermore Bookshop Mysteries series, I often use the tagline 'Agatha Christie meets Black Books' as that combined the murder mystery elements with the snarky book-centric humor.

For non-fiction, create rapport with your reader by welcoming them into your vision and showing them their future. What will their life be like once they've finished your book? Use snippets from reviews to show how your book has already changed lives. Fiction authors can also highlight reviews in their blurb – use short sentences to show that other readers are loving your book.

Workshop your blurb with other writers and test it on family and friends. Look at the structure of blurbs for other successful authors in your genre. Don't be afraid to tweak it to make it as exciting and high-stakes as possible.

Thriller/horror writer Adam Croft has a great book on writing 'killer' blurbs (I see what you did there, Adam). I also recommend you check Miss Snark (www.misssnark.blogspot.com) – a NYC literary agent who sadly no longer blogs but has left her site live with an archive of thousands of posts where she critiques query letters (basically blurbs) with her own signature style. You will laugh so much, and by the end you will have had a more thorough lesson in writing great blurbs than I could ever give you.

OPTIMIZE YOUR BLURB FOR ONLINE SALES

Use keywords, tropes, and genre search terms in your blurb – this can help you be found in more searches, as well as alerting readers that they'll like your book. Don't go crazy, though – your blurb still needs to be enjoyable to read.

Use HTML code for bold, italics, heading levels, and line space to make your blurb easily scannable. Non-fiction titles, in particular, will often use bullet points for impact.

Some authors like to list out the other books in their series so readers can see reading order. You may find this useful to help convert readers across books in a series.

No matter your project, title + cover + blurb will get you noticed

If your readers aren't digital, then these things still matter. It's important to understand how YOUR readers choose books. For example, if you're writing poetry, you're going to be focused on getting reviews, on visual social media like

Instagram, and also looking for holidays around where your poetry is given as gifts. All these things still require a quality cover and enticing title and blurb.

HOW TO ROCK YOUR TITLE, COVER, AND BLURB:

- What's your book's title? Tell it to a couple of friends you trust and ask them what they think the book is about based on the title. If they can't guess the genre, it might be time to rethink.
- If you're going to write in a series, think about how to link your titles together with a pattern. You'll also need to come up with a series title. Again, run this past your friends or readers and see if they can guess genre.
- Search your title and series title online and make sure you're not competing with a recently-published popular book in your genre.
- Figure out your budget for book covers. Once you have this number in your head, hunt out a range of design options that fit your budget. (You need to know the budget first because this will impact what type of designer you each for – pre-made or custom). Start compiling a Pinterest board or folder of inspiration to show your designer.
- Write your blurb. Now write it again.
- WRITE YOUR BLURB AGAIN. Tear up the paper in frustration. Scream about how this writing thing isn't all it's cracked up to be. Have brilliant blurb idea in the shower.
- Workshop your blurb with other writers. You'll often find a second set of eyes will pick up things you miss. There are great blurb-critique groups on

Facebook you can join. Our crew on Rage Against the Manuscript is probably happy to help!

- Look at your whole package together. Title + cover + blurb. Do they feel as polished and professional and *suitable for your genre* as you can make them? Do they sit beside current bestsellers in your categories and look damn fine? If so, you're almost ready for prime time.

Chapter Ten

STEP 7. UPLOAD AND PUBLISH – THE NUTS AND BOLTS

This chapter is all about getting your book from a file on your desktop of a bunch of handwritten pages to a live product people can download and read.

CHOOSE YOUR FORMATS

One of the cool things about self-publishing is that it's brought back types of stories that haven't been popular before and opened doors for alternative formats to flourish. It's worthwhile considering if you might be interested in publishing across multiple formats.

First of all, you've got ebooks. I recommend even if you're after print sales, you should have an ebook because it's free to publish and you might be surprised how many people buy them. The interesting thing about the ebook is how it has enabled writers of different lengths to enjoy success.

Traditional publishers have certain word count expectations they stick to – they want novels for adults to be between 60,000-90,000 words, fantasy tomes can be up to 120,000, category romance 40-55,000, YA around 40,000-

70,000, etc. If a book falls too far out of these expected lengths, the publisher will likely pass. Too long, and the book will cost too much for the publisher to print. They'll either have to price it higher (meaning fewer people will buy it) or eat into their margins. Too short, and the book won't look like a good value to readers viewing it on a store bookshelf. They'll choose something that costs that same but gives them more story for their bucks.

But with a digital market, the length of a book isn't an immediate, tactile sensation. The price of your book is set by you, and it doesn't have to correlate to length. Because of this, authors like H. M. Ward, Hugh Howey, etc are making it big with serials. Other authors are publishing epic 250,000 science fiction tomes and raking in high pages reads in KU. Some of the top indie authors on Amazon publish short travel guides or prepper manuals. Think about how you might be able to play with length for your audience.

You can use internal links in ebooks to lead readers around the book. Authors are experimenting with pick-a-path books where the readers can make certain choices that lead to other chapters, a great idea being carried to the next level by developers of interactive fiction like the Choice of Games company.

Audiobooks are a growth area where indies are seeing a lot of success. The initial cost can be huge - $2,000-5,000 in production costs for a full-length book. If you're already doing well, audio can be a good secondary income stream. I've just signed a deal with a publisher for the audiobooks on my latest series, and I'm currently producing audio for another series myself using the website Findaway Voices. I'm enthusiastic for audio because I see it as such a huge potential for authors and because it's an accessible format that allows blind and low-vision readers a chance to access a wide library of stories.

In print, you have all the options a publisher has available. Print-on-demand often lacks the polish of a publisher, but for many types of books that doesn't matter. We've already spoken about opportunities for self-publishing in print in the previous chapter.

And then, of course, you have writers completely outside traditional book structure. Think about story apps, mixing writing with VR, anything you can imagine. My friend Felicity Banks/Louise Curtis (www.shootingthrough.net) writes interactive fiction and escape rooms. She landed the gig in part because of her track record as a fiction author.

KU OR WIDE?

This is an ebook only consideration, but as the majority of your sales will likely be digital, this is probably the most important decision you make about your book's future.

Will you put your book in Kindle Unlimited (KU)?

KU is Amazon's 'Spotify for books.' Readers love it because they can binge read as many books as they want for a set fee. For the 'whale readers' who abound in genre fiction, KU is a blessing from the Reading Gods.

For authors, KU offers three advantages:

- Access to a large pool of hungry readers, many of whom will only read KU books. Readers feel as though KU books are 'free,' so they're more likely to take a chance on a new author.
- Access to KU-only marketing features, including free days (the ability to set your book to free for five days every three months) and Kindle Countdown Deals (where you can set your book on a sale for up to 7 days and still keep 70% of the royalties, even if the book is $0.99).

- Preferential treatment in Amazon's algorithm. We know that Amazon encourages buyers to read books in KU so that they have more exclusive content than other retailers. We don't know exactly what that looks like, but it is a thing.

If you want your ebook in KU, **it must be exclusive to Amazon**. You can sell the paperback and audiobook other places, but not the ebook. Also, you don't get paid a royalty as you do for a sale. Amazon pays a tiny fraction of a cent for every 'page' a reader reads.

Amazon has an algorithm that builds a standardized page count across all books – this is called KENPC (Kindle Edition Normalized Page Count) and stops authors from using giant fonts and other formatting tricks to inflate their page count.

KU has a 'pot' of money each month (made from the money paid by KU subscribers) and Amazon divides that pot by the total pages read to arrive at their per-page-read rate. They will usually top up the pot with an influx of cash each month to keep the rate between $0.004-$0.0049 (Yup, that's less than half a cent per page).

Sounds complicated? It is. What can I say? You get used to it. When random people overhear me talking to fellow authors they must think we're talking a different language.

KU has become such a force in the marketplace that KU readers have their own trends, preferred genres, and reading habits. Tropes, genres, and cover styles that do well wide might sink in KU, and vice versa. Generally speaking, KU readers read more books per month, they read genre fiction, and they are more responsive to hot trends.

Many authors have built successful careers and multi-million dollar businesses writing for KU readers. The biggest downside is that you're only building readership in one market. You're relying solely on Amazon – if they make changes to the program or drop it (or you) completely, then your income will suffer.

Going wide (having your books available on Apple Books, B&N, Kobo, Google Play as well as Amazon) gives you more of a safety net because you spread your risk. There's also less competition on the other platforms (and you'll still be earning royalties from sales on Amazon), and if you can nail your covers and genre, you'll find your books will be 'stickier' (retain regular sales volume) for longer.

On the downside, you miss out on tapping into the voracious KU readership. In certain genres, this can make it difficult to stand out. You'll have to spread your efforts across five platforms instead of laser-focusing on Amazon only. You may find it more difficult to find readers willing to take a chance on a new author.

While success is possible on both platforms, wide usually takes longer to build. The majority of the runaway indie successes of the last five years (the six-and-seven figures a month authors) are in KU. However, many wide authors choose this path because they've seen Amazon make changes with no notice that tank an author's career overnight. They need the 'security' of an audience on the other platforms in order to keep their mental health intact.

You can do a little of both. I put new books into KU and then pull them wide after the page reads start to die down. Some authors launch wide for two weeks, then pull their books from the other platforms to place in KU. Some authors are KU in one pen-name, wide with another.

Whether you want to try KU is up to you – there is no right or wrong answer. Consider the following points:

- Are your readers in KU? If you write in a KU-

heavy genre, it's best to at least start by going
where the readers are.

- Can you deal with placing all your trust/hopes on
  Amazon?
- Can you deal with the additional hassle of
  publishing your books on multiple platforms?

Remember, your KU term only lasts 90 days, so it's worth
at least experimenting with KU to see what it's like.

GOING WIDE: DIRECT VS AGGREGATORS

If you choose to go wide, you can do it in one of two ways –
by uploading your books to each platform yourself, or by
using an aggregator.

An aggregator allows you to upload your book once. In
exchange for a percentage of your royalties, the aggregator
will then place your book on all the different sales platforms.
If you have to make changes to that book (for example,
uploading a new file to fix some typos or placing the book on
sale) you can do it from the aggregator's platform and they'll
publish the changes across all vendors.

Draft2Digital is the aggregator I use – I use them for
B&N (because you couldn't go direct as a New Zealand
author when I started self-publishing), library databases like
Hoopla and OverDrive, and some smaller marketplaces like
Tolino and Scribd. They make things super easy, and I defi-
nitely recommend them!

For Apple, Kobo, and Google Play, I'm direct. This allows
me to keep the majority of my royalties, and also allows me
access to merchandising opportunities with the individual
companies (by this I mean the vendor will promote my book.
Kobo, in particular, has an awesome dashboard of monthly

promotional opportunities you can apply for. You cannot access these through Draft2Digital).

I recommend being direct with Amazon for sure – it's likely to be your biggest earner. For the other platforms, do what you think is right for you. If I recommended one to be direct, it would be Kobo because of the promotions dashboard. Apple is my second-highest earning platform, so it's good to know I'm not giving away 10% of my royalties there.

UPLOADING TO A VENDOR

For ebooks, there are five main vendors; Amazon, Apple Books, Barnes & Noble, Kobo, and Google Play. There are also several smaller stores such as Smashwords, Tolino, and Scribd, as well as stores like OverDrive specifically for libraries.

Remember, if you opt to enroll your books in Kindle Unlimited, you must remain exclusive to Amazon. Otherwise, you should have your books on as many platforms as possible.

You'll need to sign up for an account at each vendor, and give them the required tax information and bank details so they can pay your royalties. Whether you're uploading to Amazon or Kobo or any other vendor, you're going to see roughly the same fields to fill in to upload a book. Here's what each field means.

TITLE

The title of your book. This has to match the title on your cover. Choose an exciting title that represents your genre and offers readers an enticing hint at what they might discover inside.

SUBTITLE

If you have a subtitle you can add this here. Sometimes people like to include some indication of the book's genre. For example, I sometimes use 'a paranormal reverse harem' on my romance books. On some vendors, you're only allowed to do this if the subtitle appears on your book cover.

SERIES NAME

The name of the series. For example, 'Nevermore Bookshop Mysteries.'

SERIES NUMBER

The sequence of the book in the series.

EDITION

Sometimes, you might update a book. Leave blank unless you're uploading a significant update to a book.

AUTHOR

That's you! Make sure you use the name you want to be public.

CONTRIBUTORS

Other authors, contributors, or illustrators (if you're writing a children's book). You don't have to add your cover artist or editor unless their name will mean something to your audience.

DESCRIPTION

This is your blurb. We've spoken about blurbs at length in the last chapter, so you should be good to go. Use the available formatting tools/coding to add bold, subheadings, and italics.

ISBN

This is an International Standard Book Number – an identification number used by the publishing industry to help distinguish and locate books. Each ISBN identifies the country, region, or language of the book, the publisher, the format and title.

You do not require an ISBN to self-publish, but if part of your publishing plan involves being stocked in bookstores or libraries, it might be worth considering. In your country, there will be an issuing body that takes care of allocating ISBNs. In some countries – like New Zealand, yay! – ISBNs are free, while other places will incur a small fee. You need one ISBN for each format, so a book released in ebook, print, and audio will need three ISBNs in total. If you do a second edition of your book with changes, you'll require a new ISBN.

PUBLISHER OR IMPRINT

Some vendors will allow you to add your own publishing house to this field. If you don't fill in this field, it will auto-populate with the vendor's self-publishing arm. Many indies like to invent their own publisher or imprint because it looks more professional. I have an 'imprint' for my fiction (Bacchanalia House) and one for my non-fiction (Rage Against the Manuscript).

LANGUAGE

Choose the language you've used for the majority of the book.

PUBLISHING RIGHTS

You'll be asked if you own the copyright for your work or if it's a public domain work (for example, if you're publishing *Pride & Prejudice*).

AGE / GRADE RANGE

Use this only if your book is for a junior market. Otherwise, leave it in adult even if it's YA, as many adults read YA.

ENABLE DRM

I've spoken about DRM in an earlier chapter. I always choose 'no.'

CATEGORIES

Categories are a key tool for readers to discover new authors they love. Many readers use categories to browse their favorite genre online and see which books take their fancy. For this reason, it's important to place your book in the correct categories.

On Amazon, you can only choose two categories. Some other sites allow three categories. You want to choose the categories where your readers will be most likely to search for your books.

For example, if you've written a supernatural urban fantasy, you want to put it in fiction > fantasy > urban, and maybe fiction > mystery/suspense > supernatural, and not in non-fiction > occult and supernatural. The people searching that category are looking for books on true hauntings and Wiccan rituals, not fantasy novels.

Most books will fit neatly within at least one category. For example, my books are most definitely fiction > romance > paranormal. For your second category, try to choose something different to help you get in front of a wider number of readers – instead of choosing a second romance category for my Nevermore books, I list it in a mystery category.

Choose the most specific category possible. Your book will appear in all the main branches of your category. For example, if I choose fiction > romance > paranormal > vampires, my book can be found by people browsing the general romance category AND the general paranormal category. However, if I just choose fiction > romance, readers won't find my book in the paranormal or vampire category unless I use keywords to get there.

KEYWORDS

After categories come keywords. These are words readers type into the search box to find books they might enjoy. You want to include as many potential words and phrases as possible to help readers (and the vendor's algorithms) to understand what's inside your book.

On Amazon, you have seven slots for keywords. However, you can use more than one keyword in each slot. You have 50 characters in the slot and you can use every one. Choose words readers looking for a story like yours might want to choose. Focus on the main elements and tropes in your story. You can also use keywords to get into categories you weren't able to use in your category selection, so choose as many of these as fit your book. Amazon provides a list of categories with keyword requirements in their Helpdesk section.

Kindlepreneur has a great article (https://kindlepreneur.-com/7-kindle-keywords) on how to use your keywords and choose the best ones. I recommend giving it a read.

PRE-ORDER/RELEASE NOW

You can choose to release your book as soon as the vendor approves it, or put it up for pre-order. If you choose to make a book available for pre-order, this means readers can opt to reserve a copy of the book now for a release date in the future. They will be charged on release day, and all the sales royalties for the pre-order book will hit your account on that same day.

On Amazon, you're given a boost in ranking on release day equal to around 50% of the pre-orders you have. On other vendors, the boost can be even higher. Having a popular book with a ton of pre-orders can help you rock a great launch. However, if you don't think you'll get a decent amount of pre-orders, it's usually better to wait until release day to go live on Amazon.

All the vendors that allow you to create pre-orders do them up to a year in advance without the need for a completed book. This can give you time to organize launch activities and advertising and is great for encouraging read-through on your series. The best time to convince readers to buy the next book in your series is immediately after they've finished the last book. This is how I use pre-orders. Occasionally, if I'm writing a super trendy book or if I have a certain type of promotion I'll put the pre-order for book 1 up to capture readers desperate for more in that trend.

TERRITORIES

You can decide if your book will be available worldwide or only in certain countries. This is mainly for people who may have sold the publishing rights to a certain territory but are self-publishing in the others. I'd choose 'worldwide' unless you have a compelling reason not to.

On most vendors, you're able to set country-specific pricing. Some (Amazon, Kobo) will automatically populate prices based on current exchange rates. I always go through these prices and tidy the numbers. (For example, if Canada converts to $4.72 I'll change it to $4.99, etc).

PRICE

Set the price for your book.

As we've already discussed, one of the key advantages of self-publishing ebooks is the ability to offer cheaper books to voracious readers. Amazon knows that readers buy more books during a specific price range – that's why they encourage self-publishers to price between $2.99-9.99 by offering 70% royalties. Outside of this range, a book on Amazon will only receive 35% royalties.

Ideally, you want to price as high as you can before readers stop buying your book. Many self-publishers will have their first book at $0.99 to entice people to try it. You have to sell six times as many books at $0.99 as you do at $2.99 to make the same amount of money.

Wide authors have another pricing option called Permafree. This is where you set the first book in your series permanently free, and use that as a loss leader to draw readers into your series. Permafree only works if a book is in a series, and the more cliffhangery your ending is, the better it works.

You can set your book to free on Apple, Kobo, Google

Play, and B&N, either by going direct or by using an aggregator like Draft2Digital. Amazon doesn't have an option to set your book free (unless you're in Kindle Unlimited, and you can set your book free for 5 days out of 90, but then you'd be exclusive to Amazon). You can get a book set free on Amazon by publishing it free on the other vendors. Amazon hates for other vendors to beat them on price, so they will 'price match' your book to free.

It will usually take a couple of days for Amazon to notice and match the lower price. You can hurry them along by going to the 'report a lower price' on the book's product page.

UPLOAD YOUR FILE

Here you upload your book file. Amazon uses the mobi format, while the other vendors use epub. You can upload a normal docx file formatted with styles – the uploader will convert it into mobi or epub.

The program will kick back if there are any errors in your files, but you'll want to use the preview option to make sure everything has come out the way you want it. (This is especially important for print).

UPLOAD YOUR COVER FILE

Do the thing! Make sure your cover file meets the minimum dimension requirements. For Amazon, this is 2,560 x 1,600 pixels. The minimum image **size** allowed is 1,000 x 625 pixels – that's probably gonna look a bit shit, though. The maximum image **size** allowed is 10,000 x 10,000 pixels, but you don't need to make it that big. Your **cover** image has gotta be less than 50MB.

CHECK YOUR FILES

Vendors allow you to download their files to your reading device or check on your screen. I highly recommend you take a look, especially for your print book.

PUBLISH

Hit that button. You're ready!

Most vendors advise they take around 72 hours to approve your book for publishing.

PRINT BOOKS

Now that you've been through the process with an ebook, you can transfer much of the same info over to your print version.

For print, you have two options – you can either use print-on-demand or a printing service. Print-on-demand means when someone orders your book from Amazon, Amazon (or another vendor) will then print one copy of that book and send it off to that person. You don't have to be involved in the process. You carry no inventory and you don't have to pay anything upfront – you'll see a royalty every time a reader purchases a book.

The disadvantage is that the books tend to have a more expensive list price because there are no economies of scale. You're able to order author copies of your book at cost, but if you're ordering them to sell in person, the higher production cost will eat into your potential profit margin. If you live in a country like New Zealand, far away from the print-on-demand center, you'll end up losing even more of your potential profit from shipping costs.

If you plan to hand-sell a lot of print copies at conventions, events, or shows, it might be worthwhile to do a run with a local printer. Printing 100-500 copies and storing them in your garage until you need them will mean that the per-unit cost is lower. Shipping will probably cost less, too (especially if you choose a local company), so you'll have more profit per book.

I recommend you do both if you need print copies to hand-sell. You can use the same ISBN for both versions. If you don't do events and the majority of your customers will be online (like mine), you won't need the local print run.

POD SERVICES

Several companies provide print-on-demand services. The two most commonly used by self-publishers are KDP Print and IngramSpark. Both services will manage books on Amazon, and if you tick a box for 'expanded distribution,' they will manage your POD books on other retailers world-wide and make them available to libraries and bookstores. Ticking expanded distribution will add a couple of dollars to the overall cost of producing each book.

I use KDP Print for Amazon sale only. It's super easy to use. You can create print books from the same KDP dashboard you use for ebooks, and it will pre-populate details from your ebook over to your print book (and vice versa) so you don't have to repeat everything.

Not ticking expanded distribution on Amazon allows me to get my books to a $9.99 price point while still making a few bucks in royalties. $9.99 seems to appeal to more print buyers, and I'm selling more print copies than ever.

I then upload the same book with the same ISBN to IngramSpark. I use IngramSpark for expanded distribution, but not to Amazon (because KDP Print takes care of that). I also buy author copies from IngramSpark as they are closer to me in New Zealand so it's cheaper.

This is a complex way of doing things that works for me because I'm trying to maximize profit on Amazon – my biggest platform – while also making my books available as widely as possible. It's a win/win for my specific situation. Your situation and your success metrics may vary.

For uploading your print copy to a service, most of the fields will be the same between print/ebook – title, description, categories, etc. Here are a few specific to print:

LARGE PRINT

Readers with a print disability may like to have a paperback version with a font size they can read. In certain genres, this is in hot demand – such as cozy mysteries where the audience skews older. Amazon allows you to provide this by making 'large print' an option you can use – you can link it with your other formats through Author Central and it will sync your reviews. It acts as a separate book entry and will need its own ISBN.

A good font size to use is 16-point. If you're going to do large print, opt for a large trim size. 6x9 will help keep your pages down if you usually print in 5x8. It's a good idea to have your designer add a banner or star that reads 'large print edition' on the cover.

Vellum can now auto-generate a large-print version of your print book. Otherwise, you'll need to manually format it.

INTERIOR PAPER

You can choose from black/white or color printing (color will be more expensive), and white or cream paper. I opt for cream paper because to me white looks too stark. White is the best option for books with lots of images, as it shows off color and contrast with increased vibrancy.

You'll have to let your cover designer know your paper choice because white/cream papers have a different thickness (called GSM) that will slightly change the width of your book's spine.

You cannot change this once you've published.

TRIM SIZE

This is the size of your book. Novels have standard trim sizes for trade paperbacks – most are 5x8, 5.25x8, 5.5x8.5, or 6x9. If your novel is shorter, try a smaller size so it has more pages. If your novel is longer, try a larger size so it's less bulky.

Manuals and workbooks are usually larger – 8x10, 8.5x11. General non-fiction is usually 6x9. Kids' picture books are 8x10 or 10x8, but can be a whole range of sizes. Artbooks can be whatever size you want. In fact, any book can be whatever size you want – I'm just trying to help you narrow it down.

You cannot change this once you've published.

BLEED

'Bleed' is how close images get to the edge of the page. If you have images that reach right to the edge of the pages, add bleed to your book so that your images don't end up with a white border around them when the book is trimmed. For a 6x9 book, you'd usually set bleed to around 6.125x9.25. Talk to your designer if you're feeling confuzzled.

You cannot change this once you've published.

COVER TYPE

You'll usually have two options – matte or glossy. Glossy is a shiny surface. If your cover has a lot of black, this will make it look darker. It will often make artwork appear more striking. Children's books and non-fiction and anything art will usually go gloss. Matte doesn't have the sheen and looks quite sophisticated. It's typical for novels/fiction/poetry books.

You cannot change this once you've published.

EXPANDED DISTRIBUTION

Tick if you want your book to be distributed to library and bookstore catalogs, as well as to other online retailers (but just because it's distributed does not mean it will be purchased).

AUDIO

Audiobooks are the fastest-growing segment of the publishing market. It's definitely worth considering getting your books in audio if you think there's a market for your words. People are now streaming audio to their devices and listening to audiobooks on Echo and Google Home. There are audio subscription packages similar to KU, and with Amazon's Whispersync, you can read your book at a coffee shop, then when you hop into your car the audio will start playing from the page you finished reading. It's so rad.

Right now, there's an opportunity to stand out in audio because there isn't as much selection as there is for print and ebooks. There are a few different options for audio – the main two used by indies are ACX and Findaway Voices. These act both as production houses (helping to pair you up with a narrator and manage the recording of your book) and as distribution (getting your book onto the platforms and managing royalties).

On ACX, you're able to choose a narrator with the following two options – you can pay the full amount of the production (an amount per finished hour) upfront and keep the entire royalty. Or you can pay nothing upfront and split the royalties with your narrator.

On Findaway Voices, you have the option of paying for the full production up front, or if your book qualifies, you'll be able to pay half upfront and pay for the other half by splitting the royalties until the remainder of the bill is paid. The difference between this and the ACX royalty split is that on ACX the narrator would get 50% of the royalties as long as the audiobook was sold. If you have a hit, they could end up earning a significant amount. That's their incentive for choosing royalty split.

You can also create the audiobook yourself (either by hiring your own narrator or narrating yourself) and upload it to your chosen platform.

If using ACX, you'll also need to decide if you want to be exclusive. This gives you higher royalties, but means your books won't be available anywhere else apart from Amazon, Audible, and iTunes. Findaway Voices distributes to a number of other retailers. It's up to you which you think is best.

HOW TO ROCK MAKING YOUR BOOK LIVE:

- Decide which formats you'll use for launch. Ebook and print should be a must. Anything else?
- KU or wide – what's your poison?
- If you're going wide, choose which platforms you'll be using directly. If you're like me and you live in

New Zealand, you may find that sometimes the choice is made for you.

- Lockdown book information like your title, subtitle, description, series name, etc.
- Sort yourself some ISBNs if you're gonna use 'em.
- Choose your two categories. Choose them well.
- Find keywords relevant to your readership.
- Decide if you're doing a pre-order. You'll need to have a cover and blurb prepared to upload immediately.
- Upload – get to know the process for each format on the different quirks of each system.
- Pick your pricing strategy for book 1/your whole series. Reserve the right to change your mind later.
- Check everything is A-OK before you hit publish! Check it again! You want this launch to be perfection!

Chapter Eleven

STEP 8. LAUNCH WITH A BANG!

Your book launch is the best marketing tool you have. Reader interest is always highest during the launch, so you should take advantage of this and do a big marketing push.

This is when you need to take off your author and publisher hats, and put on your fancy-schmancy marketing hat. It can be hard to think like a marketer when you have no marketing background. You don't want to be scammy. You don't want to 'bother' people.

Remember that you're only bothering people if you're contacting them out-of-the-blue asking them to buy a book they have no interest in. Marketing isn't like that these days – no one wants to waste time or money or energy on people who don't want our shit. What we do now is wait for people to indicate "this is something I'm interested in" and then we can say, "Oh, that's so cool! Me too. You might like my book."

There are people in the world who are genuinely waiting for exactly the book you've created. Think about how excited you are when you hear your favorite author has released a new book. You're grateful you heard about the release so you can grab it RIGHT NOW. That's how people feel about your book. Isn't that awesome?

Telling people who are interested in your work that you've got something new out isn't scammy. Trying to convince people who AREN'T interested that they need your book, over and over again – that *is* scammy. Telling them you've written a book and then selling them a toaster – that might be scammy, or just plain odd. You? Not scammy.

So don't worry so much. And remember that as much as this marketing stuff can seem a little foreign, it's how you get to connect with readers – which is basically the most fun thing about being an author apart from the actual writing bit.

First, you need to decide what day to launch. You don't need to put too much thought into this beyond making sure the book is actually finished :) Do try to steer clear of public and school holidays. During these times people are busy with family and other commitments and aren't paying attention to new books.

Design your launch around your readers. Focus on activities that will alert any current audience you have about your book, and that will bring in new readers interested in your title.

Here are some things to consider:

- What formats do you want to launch with? Ebook, print, audio, other formats like workbooks or large print.
- Will you do a pre-order? Only some platforms allow pre-orders. I have found in my experience that on Amazon they are great for next-in-series but not for first in a new series or standalone. On the other platforms, they are great for all books.
- Do you need to hire someone or coordinate other people/details? For example, are you using a

publicist? Are you doing a collaborative launch with another author? Do you need to wait for your cover designer to finish book 2's cover so you can put that up for pre-order first?

PREPARING FOR LAUNCH

Here are a few activities you should do before your book launches.

CLAIM YOUR BOOK IN AUTHOR CENTRAL

Author Central is a hub for your books on Amazon. It gives you an author page – when a reader clicks on your name, they'll see a list of your books, a bio, and a feed of news and social media posts. Making an Author Central page is a simple way to increase your visibility and sell-through on Amazon.

To create an Author Central page, you'll need to sign up your pen name to authorcentral.amazon.com. Then, upload your books. You need to create a page in each territory – US, UK, AU, FR, etc – add your books, a bio, author photo, and links to social media/blog feeds for news.

CREATE A MULTILINK

It gets really tedious writing out every store link for your book every time you talk about it. Added to this problem, if you send readers to an Amazon page outside their territory (for example, if you give the US link to readers in Australia) it will look as though your book isn't available. Multilinks solve this issue, as well as allow you to gather additional information.

I use Books2Read.com (www.books2read.com) to create

my links. There are lots of other companies that provide links specifically for authors (ReaderLinks is another one I've seen around). I like Books2Read because they're affiliated with Draft2Digital, who are awesome.

ADD YOUR LINKS TO YOUR AUTHOR WEBSITE AND SOCIAL MEDIA

Got your multilink? Good – now make a page for your book on your website and direct readers where to grab it!

SEND OUT AN ARC TO REVIEWERS

Early reviews can be one factor in a book's success. Social proof is an important part of the psychology of shopping – we like to purchase things and read books that others already love because it makes us feel as though we're in a super-secret club. We trust the opinions of others – even people we don't know – to point us towards things we'll enjoy.

If a reader sees a book already has several 4-5 star reviews, they'll know other people have read and enjoyed that book, and it'll make them more likely to take a chance on it even if they've never read your books before.

If they land on your author page and see no reviews, they might assume your book isn't worth their time. That's why it's a good idea to focus some of your pre-launch efforts on building a team of reviewers who could be counted on to place reviews as soon as your books come out.

Some promotion companies (such as BookBub) need to see reviews on a book before you can book their services. There's also evidence that the number and quality of reviews count toward ranking and algorithmic advantages on some of the stores (where and how much is a mystery).

In the first instance, you could talk to friends or family members who read in your genre and ask if they'd be interested in being an advance reader. You want to make sure these are amazing supportive people because you need those first reviews to land on your book to be 4-5 stars.

(NB: Sometimes, Amazon will remove reviews if they conclude they've come from friends and family – ie. reviews from people who are your friends on Facebook. It's always best to try to cultivate reviewers from readers, but we all have to start from somewhere.)

If there are reader groups or forums for your genre, you may collect a few advance readers by posting there.

You might also like to chat with other author friends who write in the same genre and might be interested in a review swap. Personally, I feel a conflict of interest as an author writing product reviews on other books, so I don't do it. Other authors don't feel that way, so you may find someone excited to swap reviews with you.

There are also ARC (advance reader copy – industry jargon for the manuscript sent out to advance readers) services and sites like Hidden Gems (www.hiddengemsbooks.com) and Booksprout (www.booksprout.co) that connect readers and reviews. These are often booked far in advance but can be a good option to get a strong influx of reviews.

I built my ARC team through my newsletter funnel. When readers sign up to my newsletter, they receive a welcome email and a link to a free story or bonus scene. Then a few days later they'd receive a second email with some fun facts about me. A few days after THAT, they get an email asking if they'd like to join my ARC team. They'd get to read books for free a week before they're published, as long as they agree to write an honest review. After I had a certain number of reviewers, I took away the email. Now, I only add new people to the team if they specifically contact me to ask.

There are specific rules on Amazon about reviews. You cannot pay people to review your books. However, you are allowed to pay for a service to help you find reviewers, such as the ones I've already mentioned. Any site that guarantees a certain number of reviews with a certain star-rating is running afoul of Amazon's TOS and could put your account in danger. Beware!

I used to manage my ARC requests manually, attaching and emailing a file with a personal message to everyone who replied. I'd send a reminder to review on the publication day, and another a week or two after that. Now I use a company called BookFunnel (www.bookfunnel.com) to manage my ARCs. It costs $20 a month and auto-sends the reminder messages. It's awesome!

There are other ways to gain reviews without an ARC team, but they usually cost money or effort. NetGalley is a site mainly used by traditional publishers to connect with book bloggers. It can be expensive to join (authors use co-ops to share a yearly subscription and save money), but will result in a trickle of reviews, sometimes from quite prestigious publications.

There are also blog tour companies that set up a tour for you around different book blogs. Many offer book reviews from bloggers as part of these tours, and some even offer review-only tours.

How many reviews is the right number? The answer to that question depends widely on what stage you're at in your author career, how many reviews similar books in your genre have, what readers expect from reviews, etc, etc. Some reviews are better than none, and better quality/higher star reviews are better than more reviews.

Ultimately, you should be looking to cultivate your own ARC team. Occasionally I have bloggers and reviewers asking me if they could join my team. I add them to the list.

ENDORSEMENTS/BLURBS

Endorsements are those little phrases on the front of a book from another author in your genre. They can be pretty tough to get if you're a brand new author, and most self-published authors don't worry about them. However, if you happen to be friends with a big name in your genre and they're supportive of your work, ask them if they'd consider writing a blurb for you. You've got nothing to lose and everything to gain!

WHAT YOU CAN DO DURING YOUR LAUNCH?

Immediately after you hit publish, you'll have to wait anywhere from 20 minutes to 3 days for your book to go live on the various storefronts. Once you see your pretty book is live, you should probably first purchase a copy and check that it all looks good – that all the chapters are present and accounted for. Then, if you haven't already done so, you'll want to update your multilink and website (if you have one... hint: you should have one!) with a page for your book and a BUY NOW button. After that, you can start putting your launch plan into action.

Probably you started your launch plan well before your launch (hint: you should do this). When you plan your launch, you want to think about it as having two key parts:

1. Current audience. Make sure anyone who has followed any of your endeavors over the years knows you have a book out. The truth is that not all your readers are constantly following your social media, waiting with bated breath for the next release. You have to shout out loud multiple times to make sure they see you have a book.

2. New readers. Every launch you do should reach a
    few more new readers than the last, and you then
    funnel those readers into your new book and then
    into your fan audience.

Here are some activities you can try during your launch.

FOR YOUR CURRENT AUDIENCE:

- Post about your book on all your social media. I'm
  not just talking one single post. I mean multiple
  posts across *at least* a two week period – telling
  people all sorts of things about the launch, sharing
  excerpts, telling them about the research you've
  done, asking them questions (this is the best thing
  because people just want to talk about themselves
  on social media), and getting them to play silly
  games. I usually get the best engagement from
  polls or from predictive text games. Make of that
  what you will.
- Another thing I like to do in my Facebook group is
  to create a 'spoiler discussion thread' for people
  who've read the book to talk about all their feels.
  This works really well because my books end on
  whopper cliffhangers so readers have opinions and
  theories.
- Boost a FB post or run Facebook ads on your
  mailing list – if you export your mailing list then
  import to Facebook, the ad platform can find most
  of those people with accounts and serve ads to
  them. These ads specifically tell your current
  audience that a new book is live.
- Run a competition. This competition will go up on

all your social media and on your mailing list.
Because readers are eager to have something for
free, you'll have a higher rate of engagement,
ensuring more of your current readers (and also
possibly new readers, too) will see you have a new
book out. I love doing big swag packs with hand-
picked goodies I've chosen based on the theme or
setting in my book. When running competitions,
it's important to follow the applicable laws in your
country (for example, it's usually illegal to require
people to show proof of purchase to enter a
competition).

- Write a prequel and give it away for free on Prolific
  Works and/or BookFunnel and/or your website
  and/or the vendors as a permafree. This can also be
  used to entice new readers to get excited about
  your series.

- Add a link to your book in your email signature.
  Again, this could be seen by potential new readers
  who contact you, too, but it serves as a reminder
  to anyone you email regularly.

- Host an in-person event. Consider this carefully, as
  you may end up spending a lot of money on a
  venue, food, entertainment, etc, but not make up
  much in sales. Events and book launches are
  usually attended by your family and friends. It's a
  celebration for you and all the hard work of getting
  your book out. In terms of sales, they work best if
  you have a large existing audience and can build an
  event around the launch that isn't just 'mingle and
  talk about my book.' Entice your fanbase in with
  entertainment, great speakers, etc, then hit 'em
  with your book table as soon as they come in the
  door. Another way to sell books is to raise your

ticket price but give every ticket holder a free
book.

FOR NEW READERS:

- Contact local media about your books. Remember
  that writing a book isn't news. You need to tie it to
  a wider interest story. I received lots of media for
  my children's picture book because I tied it into
  statistics about bullying in schools and my own
  experiences.
- Put together a leaflet showcasing your book and
  hand it out to local libraries. You may also need to
  look at listing your books with companies that sell
  into libraries. Making librarians aware of your
  book can help you get stocked and encourage them
  to talk you up to their patrons.
- Put an earlier book in your series on sale. I will
  often put book 1 in a series free or on sale for
  $0.99 during book 3 or 4's launch. I will then use
  newsletter services like BookBub, Booksends,
  Bargain Booksy, The Fussy Librarian, etc, to let
  potential new readers know the book is on sale.
- Run Facebook ads or AMS ads. PPC ads allow you
  to target readers who like a similar book or
  fandom. For example, when I launched a new book
  in the Nevermore Bookshop Mysteries series –
  which features the character James Moriarty from
  the Sherlock Holmes books – I targeted fans of the
  BBC Sherlock series. I wrote ad copy that said
  things like, "What to read about Sherlock..." These
  were my most successful ads because they spoke
  directly to an existing fanbase.

- Post in Facebook groups for your genre. This technique works best when you're already an active member of the groups and you create discussions with lots of engagement.
- Social media takeovers. During these events, you will go to another author's social media page (with their permission, obviously) and 'take it over' with your own posts, games, and competitions. Their readers will participate, and if your book appeals, they may give it a try. The more closely your books align, the more readers you'll likely pick up from takeovers.
- Online parties. Similar to takeovers but hosted on your own social media profiles, you'll invite other writers to come along to do games and competitions. They'll bring along a few of their readers each time, and in between their takeovers you can do your own games and promote your own books.
- Ask other authors in your genre to promote your book to their readers. Collaborating with other authors in your genre is one of the quickest ways to build new fans. Self-publishing isn't a zero-sum game – a reader can enjoy my book and also a book by my friend. They read so much they don't have to choose. I link her new release in my newsletter and she does the same to me. We all win. The ability to build these support networks with other authors in your genre is why it's a good idea to start participating online before you launch.
- Set up podcast interviews. A great idea for non-fiction authors in particular, but it would work equally well for fiction. Find podcasts that talk about subjects related to your books. For example,

true crime podcasts might be a great fit not just
for true crime books, but for mystery writers.
Contact the hosts and ask if they'd be interested in
having you as a guest. Talk up how awesome you
are and say that you've just released a book. It also
helps if you're a fan of the show and can gush
about it.

- Create YouTube content. YouTube is where most
  people are finding online content these days.
  Create videos about aspects of your book and
  upload them, with a link to your book in the notes,
  of course! This works great for non-fiction authors
  who are teaching something that will improve a
  reader's life. Poets might like to set their poems to
  music (even cooler if it's music you've created) and
  post live clips from slams.

- Court bookstagrammers. Bookstagrammers and
  booktubers are readers who create amazing still
  life imagery of book covers or talk about their
  favorite books online. There are also unboxings,
  where readers will order a stack of books and video
  themselves opening them. Some PR companies
  manage bookstagram campaigns for you, but you
  may prefer to find potential partners yourself.

A NOTE ABOUT PAID ADVERTISING

There are two main types of paid advertising authors do for
their books.

Discount newsletter advertising: Many services offer
readers the ability to sign up for a daily email of free or
discounted books in their genre. BookBub is the largest and
most successful – their featured book ads can cost upwards of
$500, but you're likely to sell thousands of books. But there's

also Bargain Booksy, Booksends, The Fussy Librarian, etc. As an author, you can pay a fee to have your free or discounted book pushed out to these readers on a certain date. To be included, your book has to be discounted, and it needs to be approved by the newsletter organizer.

PPC (pay-per-click) advertising: These are Amazon, Facebook, and BookBub ads. (Yes, the same Bookbub that runs paid newsletter ads also does PPC advertising. They have some really other cool features, too, such as free author profiles readers can "follow" that will send out an email when you have a new release. You should totally set yourself up as an author on Bookbub just for that). They aim to introduce your book to new readers, and you don't have to run a discount to use these ads, making them great for a launch. You can target readers who like similar authors (or even TV shows in the case of Facebook ads – you have lots of options) and you'll only be charged when someone clicks on your ad.

It's easy to waste a lot of money with PPC ads. My advice is to look at paid ads as something to add to an already successful launch. In the long-term, you're going to want to learn how to run great ads, so you might like to experiment with a small budget.

Check out Adam Croft on the Creative Penn podcast (https://www.thecreativepenn.com/2016/02/15/facebook-ads-adam-croft) and Brian D. Meeks' *Mastering Amazon Ads* book if you're ready to get started thinking about ads.

BUILDING AN AUDIENCE BEFORE YOU LAUNCH

Some authors will launch a new book on a brand new pen name and see it rocket straight to the top of the Amazon store. You can't count on this, of course. Remember my adage – I choose to believe I'm not going to be the exception.

If you're a brand new author and you want to make the

biggest splash with the launch of your book, then you might want to start finding ways to build an audience *before* you launch. That way, you already know that as soon as you hit publish you'll have at least a few rabid fans ready to snap up your book. If your audience is big enough, it could give you a serious bump on Amazon that could result in the platform working to promote you to even *more* new readers.

Pre-building an audience sounds like a great idea!

In theory.

In reality, if you're not naturally marketing savvy and you're not already involved in audience-building activities (such as a non-fiction author on the speaker circuit) it can be rage-inducing.

If the thought makes you want to break out in hives, you don't have to do it. (Remember, if it's not fun, what's the point?) But if you think you could benefit from building an audience pre-launch, here are some ideas.

The key to any successful pre-launch is two-fold.

1. Give them free content they can devour *right now*.
2. Give them a way to opt-in for *more* content in such a way that you capture information about them.

What kind of free content could you give away? Fiction authors will usually do either a sample of the book or a prequel short story. Non-fiction authors will use some book content to create a short guide. Poets can, of course, give away some poems, or perhaps an essay or video on the inspiration or themes behind the upcoming collection. Children's book authors will often do activity pages.

Free content could also include a podcast series relating to the topic of your book, Facebook posts in a private or public group, YouTube videos, or guest blog posts on popular websites. You are limited only by your imagination and your available time/resources. Also, try and keep your free content closely tied to your actual book.

Below, I give you some more ideas.

Non-fiction: If you're releasing a non-fiction book on a certain topic, the best thing you can do is to create a ton of free content about that topic – a website full of articles, a podcast, a YouTube channel. From that free content, give interested people a link to sign up for a mailing list to be notified when your book comes out.

Fiction: Fiction is a bit harder to create an audience before the book releases. One way writers do this is to put the book up for pre-order – this can work exceptionally well if your book is in a super-hot genre. You could also create a mailing list and give away a prequel story or sample of the book.

You can also adopt the same technique as for non-fiction and put up free content with links to join a mailing list. This works well for books with a theme you can speak about. For example, if you're writing a certain type of fantasy book, you could create a YouTube channel where you review other books in your genre or create content around that genre (book lists and top tens are popular on YouTube).

Poetry: Poetry has been experiencing a renaissance, fueled by social-media-savvy poets like Brian Bilston, Rupi Kaur, and my personal favorite, Nikita Gill. These 'instapoets' are largely traditionally published and account for 47% of poetry book sales in the US (https://selfpublishingad-vice.org/self-publishing-poetry-books/).

If you want to get noticed as a poet, it's a good idea to use social media as a platform. Combine your poetry with imagery to create shareable images. You can do a lot with poetry and music and video.

Allow and encourage your fans to repost and share your content. Include your social media handle on everything.

Remember when you're on social media to adhere to the brand you've created for yourself – create a cohesive poetry experience so readers feel welcomed and comfortable returning to hear your beautiful words.

RAPID RELEASE

Rapid release is a launch technique made popular by authors like Michael Anderle and Craig Martelle of the 20Books-To50k Facebook group (https://www.facebook.-com/groups/20Booksto50k/). The idea is that the closer together you release books, the more voracious readers you'll capture as they'll be able to immediately binge your series. Also, because Amazon favours newly released books and gives a ranking boost to a new release in its first 30-90 days, many authors find getting more books out during this window will help.

Rapid release means holding back on releasing books until you have several complete, then releasing them at once. BOOM BOOM BOOM.

Usually, authors will hold back 3 books to release either simultaneously (all on the same day) or in succession (once a week or every 2-3 weeks). You might have the 4th book in the series on pre-order and be writing it while you release the others.

I've heard of authors stockpiling as many as 7 books for rapid release. It can be a great way to jumpstart a successful brand. The downside is that you will spend a lot of time writing and editing without earning while you stockpile, and if your books end up fizzling (which does happen) you might have invested all that time writing a long series that didn't do well. If you'd know six months earlier the series wouldn't land, you might have adjusted the plot of your series to finish it in 3 books instead of 7.

HOW TO ROCK YOUR BOOK LAUNCH:

- Psych yourself up. Put on a wicked soundtrack of awesome tunes that'll melt your face off. You wrote a book – and that's amazing! – and now you are gonna bring it to the world!
- Make a plan. Decide all the things that need deciding – pre-order or no pre-order. KU or wide. Formats for launch? How will you get reviews? What will you focus on?
- Find your ARC reviewers if you're using them, and send them your book!
- What's your budget for your launch? You can do lots of awesome work on a launch budget of nil. I frequently launch books into the top 3,000 on Amazon with a $0 budget. I have an established audience, so there's that, but by-and-large I've built that audience without spending a ton of money. So don't feel as though you have to spend money. But if you have money to spend, you need to know how much it is so you can put it to the best use.
- Do the things on your launch – contact book reviewers, local newspapers, libraries, Facebook groups, and anyone else you think might be interested. Prioritize the stuff on your list according to what's easiest to do and what will create the biggest impact, and just... do the thing.
- Connect with other authors in your genre. Is there a way you can work together to promote each other's books?
- Create a plan for two weeks' worth of social media posts – one week before launch, one week of

launch. You can do more, but that's a good start. You can write and schedule them all in advance if you want to. (I'm rarely that organized).

- Make some graphics for your social media. You can just use your cover photo, but you might like to make some other graphics, too. Try Canva (www.canva.com) for free templates – I love to use funny quotes from the book for Instagram posts. Authors also love graphic sites like Mockup Shots (www.mockupshots.com) and Book Brush (www.bookbrush.com) – you upload your book cover and it will add it to lots of awesome images and ad templates.
- Book any promo sites you intend to use.
- Send out a newsletter to remind everyone your book is coming soon.
- It's launch day! Do a dance! Drink or eat something delicious! Put on your awesome soundtrack! And don't forget to send a newsletter to your readers and remind your ARC team to leave their reviews.
- Update your website and anywhere else you need with your live book link.
- If you've organized an in-person event, you should probably attend it. Wear something fierce. Smile a lot. Don't apologize every time someone congratulates you – you wrote a book and you deserve praise!
- It's a week later! Do another reminder to your ARC team to leave their reviews. Bask in the glory of published authordom.
- Start writing your next book.

Chapter Twelve

STEP 9. GIVE YOUR AUDIENCE SOMEWHERE TO CONGREGATE

Now that you've put a book out into the world, you're going to start acquiring readers.

This may happen slowly, or you may suddenly discover yourself in possession of many readers and no clue what to do with them.

After readers have read a book they love, what do they want to do?

- Discuss it with other readers.
- Go all giggly and fan-person over the writer.
- Find out if there's anything else in that world they can devour, or failing that, any other books by the same writer they can enjoy.

To grow your audience and to build a successful career, you need to create a *place* where your readers can go after they finish your book to find out more and hang out with you. This is good for you because the more you engage readers between releases, the more likely you'll 'convert' them into fans who buy everything you write.

The internet makes this incredibly easy. You can build an online community on the cheap – it doesn't cost anything to start a Facebook group or a mailing list. It also means you don't have to leave the house and socialize with strangers in person – a fact for which I am eternally grateful.

Some books will tell you, 'you need a Facebook group,' 'you've got to be on Twitter!' or 'Instagram is the next big thing for authors!' I'm *not* going to tell you that, because I don't think it matters so much what platform you choose for your reader community. It's more important **that you have one**, and that you learn to be a community facilitator who can make that space feel safe and fun and engaging for your crew.

A friend of mine once said to me, "people are on social media because they want to talk about themselves." This is SO TRUE and it completely changed the way I viewed my social media engagement. Instead of just giving announce-ments, I try to give my readers a chance to talk about them-selves in a way they couldn't outside my community. I give them a space they feel they need to be themselves and to be heard.

What kind of space could you create for your readers?

- A website – A website is a hub for your online presence, as well as a point of information for readers wanting to know more. Your website will list your published books, any in-person appearances, a bio about you, and contact information (you don't have to make your email address available to readers, but it's good to have some way for people to contact you in case a publisher wants to offer you a six-figure book deal). It might also include bonus content, like deleted scenes or a fan shop.

- A social media profile – Here's the thing about social media – it feels as though it's all about you posting pictures of your WIP or your dinner or your cats or whatever, but actually if you want to be really good at social media you need to make your profile *about your readers*. Choose whichever platform you enjoy – because if it feels like a chore then that'll come through. No matter which platform you choose, the rules are the same – the more interaction you have on your profile the more you'll be seen and shown to new readers and the more your reach will grow. How do you get readers to interact? MAKE IT ABOUT THEM. Ask questions that get them to talk about themselves. Run competitions that encourage answers. Play interactive games. Give them polls and ask for their opinion. Show them what you're creating FOR THEM. Issue challenges. Share their posts and replies (with permission).
- A fan group – A fan group is a community space where readers can post about their love of a book, ask questions, discuss spoilers, and maybe win stuff or get cool bonuses. As of the date of publication, most fan groups are on Facebook because that's where readers spend a significant portion of their time online. (This is the reason FB ads for readers are still so effective). This may change, and many authors do well with fan groups on other platforms.
- A mailing list – This is more of an old-school thing, but many authors still get insane engagement from readers through their mailing list. It's also one of the best things to build because unlike a social

media page where algorithms could change in a flash, you own the data.

BUILDING A MAILING LIST

A strong, reader-focused mailing list will be one of your best assets. There are three reasons for this:

- Email is a direct line into your readers' lives. You don't have to rely on them going to FB and seeing your ads or heading over to your website. You can hit them in a place they check every day.
- Your mailing list is owned and operated by you. You may use a provider to send the emails but the actual list – the data – is yours. That's powerful because it means you're not at the whims of Amazon or Facebook or Instagram changing policies or visibility.
- Email newsletters have a high conversion rate. They are one of the cheapest and easiest ways to reach the people who've already decided they like you. One of the key inbound marketing principles is that it's much easier to sell something to a person who likes you. That's why newsletters work so well.

There's no right way to do newsletters. You can do something totally basic – a link in the back of your book for anyone wanting updates, and then you just send a quick email every time you publish a book. Great! That's still 10x better than not having a mailing list in the first place.

Or you can get more complex and use automation sequences, groups, drip campaigns, freebies, A/B testing, and other marketing tools to make your newsletter super effective. I don't want to get into that too much here because it's a whole other topic. But I do want to touch on the bare basics of setting up a newsletter.

I've outlined five steps. If you can knock off all five of these, then you'll have a functioning newsletter you can send out whenever you have a new release. This is the absolute basic bare-bones of what you'll want to do, and I think anyone can achieve this. Anything extra you do is up to your skill level and enthusiasm.

Here's what you need to do:

- Decide what you want – how often to send your newsletter, what's it going to contain, regular or sporadic, what will it look like?
- Choose your platform – I use a platform called MailerLite. Many authors like Mailchimp, Sendsy, ConvertKit, or SendinBlue. There are lots of options, and most allow you to build a small list for free.
- Build your initial emails – use the templates on your platform to create a sign-up sequence to conform to privacy laws.
- Create a form – so people can sign up.
- Stick your form lots of places! – on your website, as a pop-up, at the beginning and end of your books.

That's it! You've set up a newsletter. Now you're ready to send out emails.

First, a note about where to promote your newsletter. At the minimum, you should place a link at the front and back of your books. People have tested this and found that the best places to capture readers are in the front of your book and at the end, right after you've written THE END – don't even make them turn the page, just give them the link. You can test this on your books and see where you get the best results.

You should also have your website signup ALL OVER YOUR WEBSITE. You can't go too nuts here. Seriously, some people have websites that are literally JUST their form. This is okay. You can also do a floating popup that appears when a person clicks on your site. I know they're annoying, but people use them because they're so effective.

You can also add your newsletter link to your Amazon author bio, talk about it in your reader group or on social media. Put it on the back of your business cards. Get it tattooed. Go nuts.

NEWSLETTER CONTENT

Right now, you've got a basic bare-bones organic newsletter. Readers will discover the link at the back of your books and sign up. You'll contact them when you have a new release. It will grow slowly but steadily, and you'll see some okay results.

What if you created the kind of newsletter readers are excited to get in their inbox? What if you could get more readers to open your newsletter every time you sent it and read more of your books? You want to encourage as many readers as possible to sign up because your newsletter makes them feel special and happy and amazing. And while they're at it, they will buy all the things.

Authors usually use a freebie to encourage more readers to sign up for their newsletter. You've got lots of different options for the freebie you create. Some of the most popular include:

- Prologue
- Companion novella
- An entire book

- An extended epilogue (A little tip from me to you, call it a bonus scene – readers will tear you a new one in the reviews if you call it an epilogue)
- Bonus scenes from anywhere in the book. I love to do these from another character's POV. Readers especially love sex scenes from the guy's POV.
- Extended or deleted scenes, like movie extras
- Alternate endings
- Character interviews
- Detailed family trees
- Maps or other visuals of the world
- Behind-the-scenes secrets
- Activity sheets for children's books
- A bonus video or audio download

With freebies, you can also use sites like BookFunnel or Prolific Works for delivery and to help get your freebie noticed by more people.

Now that you've got readers on your list, what will you talk to them about and how often will you email? These decisions differ for every author. Experiment and test.

I will say that one important function of your newsletter is to make sure readers don't forget about you. If you're a writer publishing one book a year, then emailing out once every 1-2 months is a great way to keep readers interested between releases, especially if you've got sneak peeks or bonus content or competitions.

I try to send out my newsletter once per week. I find that because I release so frequently I have a lot of news and content to share. I don't do a specific day because I can't handle the structure.

As for what to write about, here are some ideas:

- New releases

- Pre-orders
- Cover reveals. Cover reveals are great exclusive content, and a good excuse to email and mention an upcoming release.
- Special price promotions, such as a book on sale for $0.99. Sometimes I don't bother sending these out so readers don't get in the habit of waiting for sales. I use sales to hook new readers.
- Author events
- Launch of new formats (eg. paperback or audio now available)
- Giveaways
- Bonus content
- Games. A lot of my author friends are using sites like BuzzFeed to make quizzes about their books (which hero is for you? What book to read next?)
- Recipes, especially if they relate to the book in some way. I had a book that was about a bakery owner and the month of launch I sent out emails with recipes from the bakery. Those were really popular!
- Link to blog posts. For example, I wrote a blog post about priest holes in English castles and linked that in my newsletter because there's a naughty scene in a priest hole in my book.
- Book recommendations

Some writers also like to include personal stories about themselves, such as discussion about TV shows, the writing life, pets, thoughts about the genre, etc.

If that all sounds overwhelming and complicated, don't worry about it. If it's not fun for you, don't do it. Personally, I get a kick out of making awesome stuff for readers, but you might prefer to focus your energy on writing the next book.

HOW TO ROCK YOUR AUDIENCE:

- Think about where your peeps hang out. What platforms do they use? Are they on FB, Instagram, Discord, Slack, or Twitch?
- Think about where you enjoy hanging out online. Can you find a way to make a welcoming space for readers? Choose your social media/fan group profiles based on an intersection of what your readers like and what you enjoy.
- Build a simple website and add all your books. Urgh, I know. It's annoying. But once it's done you won't have to do it again. Hopefully forever. Or at least until the internet no longer exists. Wordpress and Squarespace are good platforms to try.
- Make a mailing list. Urgh, I know. It's also annoying. But once it's done you won't have to do it again. Well, you will have to update it and send out mail to your readers, but how much and how often is up to you. Do what feels comfortable for you.
- Ask questions and get readers to talk about themselves. This will improve your engagement and make your social media platforms more popular.
- Enjoy talking with your readers! They are awesome people who think you're just the coolest person. It's a nice ego trip. You are a rockstar of words!

Chapter Thirteen

STEP 10. USE YOUR BOOK AS A PLATFORM

You've done it! You're an author. A rockstar of words. (A wordstar, if you will). You have a book that you've written out in the world. That's actually amazing. Now, when people ask you what you've been up to at a party, you can say, "Well, I just published this book," and whip out a copy to show them.

Totally not weird at all.

Right now, you're probably focused hard on trying to get more people to buy your book. That's great. But don't over-look the advantages that being a real author might offer you in other areas of your life, especially if your ultimate goal is to be a full-time author or if you've written a book that relates to your career.

Being a published author will promote you as an expert. Imagine walking into a job interview and being able to say, "Oh, I wrote a book on this subject." Imagine a recruiter Googling your name and seeing your book on Amazon with lots of glowing reviews!

Many business owners write a book as part of their strategic plan as it will lead directly to new clients. You can use your book to source leads that you'll nurture and funnel into higher-priced items like coaching and courses. Your book can drive traffic and inquiries to an online shop or raise the profile of a bricks-and-mortar store.

But you don't have to be in business to get cool opportunities because you're a writer. You might be able to wrangle a profile about yourself in the local paper. You can pitch yourself to writers and readers festivals as a guest speaker. You can visit schools and get kids excited about reading. You could write articles about your favorite subject and have them published in magazines and other books.

You could expand your book's world into games, movies, swag, coloring books, and basically any other product you could imagine. I had my illustrator friend Bree design t-shirts with funny phrases from some of my Nevermore Bookshop characters for a reader shop on my website. Bree used the success of our Kickstarter campaign to launch her own tarot deck. I know other authors who've done coloring books, who've licensed their books as cartoons and movies, and who are writing interactive fiction and radio drama. The possibilities are truly endless.

If you feel called to teach what you've learned, you could help other authors navigate the world of writing craft or self-publishing, or be a ghostwriter for people who don't want to create their own books. You might provide services to authors or readers, such as editing, PR, or managing their social media. There are so many possibilities.

Your book is only the beginning.

HOW TO ROCK YOUR AUTHOR PLATFORM:

- Don't be shy about the fact you published a book. It doesn't matter what other people think of your genre – you've done something very few people ever achieve. Celebrate and talk about your experience. It's part of what makes you an interesting person.

- Your book might be only one part of your overall business plan or ultimate goal. If so, what is your ultimate goal? How does that factor into the success metric we worked out in chapter 1?

- If you're a business owner, think about how you can use your book to leverage into higher-profit and value-add products. This often includes courses, coaching, and membership sites, but it might be as simple as using your book to raise the profile of your store.

- Add your book to your resume and LinkedIn page. (If it's relevant to your industry). Add it to your professional and personal social media bios. Enjoy the feeling of 'published author' on your tongue.

- Think about the kinds of things you'd like to do as a writer. Do you have any writerly dreams, like speaking at a conference or mentoring young writers? You don't have to wait to be invited – contact a writers festival about applying to be on the bill (look for localized or genre-focused festivals for your best chance of success), and talk to local schools, writer groups and youth groups about hooking up with awesome young writers. You wanted to write a book, and you made that happen. If you want other things, make them happen, too.

- Pitch articles and excerpts from your book to magazines, journals, and websites. You can even earn a nice bit of spare change doing this.

- What other products within your book's world

might your readers enjoy? Give them something cool.

- Did I mention that you should be celebrating? Seriously. Eat an epic sandwich. Do a Snoopy dance. Buy a yacht. You're rocking it as a self-published wordstar! That's totally badass.

Chapter Fourteen

STEP 11. EXPERIMENT AND HAVE FUN!

Part of what's so amazing about self-publishing and being an indie author is the ability to pivot, try new things, and follow your imagination wherever it leads. You can start a new pen name and try a completely different genre, create multiple formats for your books, co-write or write in a shared world, or team up with other creatives to experiment with new ways of storytelling.

You can do *all the things*. This can be freeing. It can also be a lead weight around your neck, stopping you from moving forward. It can be both at the same time. Humans are complex weirdos.

Yes, do all the things if that makes you happy, but **try to stick to a plan.** There's always the temptation to chase a new shiny idea, but always put on your publisher hat and ask if that idea is going to get you closer to your ultimate success.

In 2016 I released a really successful first book in a new series. It did so well that I worked my ass off to publish a co-written book with a friend, write a standalone book in a new world, and finish another series under my other pen name. All the while, the readers of that first book were left wondering if the series will continue.

Even though I published a book every two months, it was nearly eight months later before I wrote book 2, and by that time many of those readers moved on. I don't regret those tangent projects, but splitting my focus set me back probably a year from my goal of being a full-time author. Now I finish one series before I start another, and if a shiny idea is calling to me, I might set aside an hour a day to noodle on it instead of breaking away from what I know works.

Always look for new opportunities. This year I funded a children's book on Kickstarter. I'm also signed up to release the first book in a series a chapter at a time on an app. While I focus on doing more of what works, I pay attention to what's going on in the wider self-publishing world and where I might be able to slide on in and find new readers.

Read indie books and look at how other authors manage their careers. Some of my favorite self-published authors are H. Y. Hanna (cozy mysteries), Darcy Coates (haunted house horror), Karpov Kinrade (YA vampire fantasy), C.M. Stunich (reverse harem romance), and Gala Darling (blogger extraordinaire).

And lastly, **don't be a stranger!** Reach out to the amazing community of indie authors across the world. Come join the conversation and share your journey in the Rage Against the Manuscript Facebook group (www.facebook.-com/groups/rageagainstthemanuscript). Share advice, learn from others, and commiserate over creative challenges. Writing can be a lonely pastime, and having a tribe makes it that much more fun.

How to rock being an indie author:

- Make a plan.
- Stick to the plan as much as possible...

- ...while also allowing a bit of wriggle room for the Muse.
- Keep an eye on what others are doing and how the industry changes and adapts.
- Read lots of awesome books by fellow authors. I know, what a chore, right?
- Join the conversation and use your story to inspire other authors. If we all lift together, nothing can stop us.
- Something.
- Something.
- PROFIT.
- *(Just kidding)*.
- *(Sort of)*.

Chapter Fifteen

PUTTING IT ALL TOGETHER

You may have got to this point in this book, and you're think-ing, "I've got a plan for the rest of my series and I've nailed my author brand and all that jazz, but I don't see how this is going to get me any closer to my goals."

Fair enough. That's why what I'm going to do in this chapter is to show you how all the elements in this book can come together to create the potential for an amazing writerly future.

When you go to your 9-to-5 job, you're exchanging your time for money. You work 40 hours a week and you receive a check for an agreed amount at the end. That amount is fixed – it goes up or down if you change your hours. You might get a pay raise, but generally speaking, your income will stay fixed at around the same amount.

If you have a full-time career as an author, life is very different.

Your books are infinitely scalable. What I mean by this is that you can create a business that sells 1,000 books a month, but that business could grow to sell 10,000 books a month or 100,000 books a month without you needing to do put in extra hours or hire more people. (You might choose to do those things, but if your business is scalable, the **process is the same** no matter how many copies you sell). This separates you completely from this time-for-money exchange.

You can sell ebooks and audio over and over again – there's no inventory to stock and your books will never go out of print. With POD technology, you can even create scalability for paperbacks. You can sell books all over the world, and create other formats like audio. You can license subsidiary rights (film, foreign translations).

Another thing you have at your disposal is data. All the publishing platforms give you instant, real-time access to data that shows you how book sales are going. Many traditionally-published authors don't get this visibility. They'll see a royalty statement every six months, so they can't tell what marketing efforts move books. You can see in minute detail what works and what doesn't, and use this data to improve and make tweaks.

No one owes you an audience or a living. You will rise or wither by how much you satisfy readers with your books. That uncertainty can be scary, but for the right kind of people, it's creatively stimulating.

It helps a lot if you have a partner with a normal job and one of those nice, regular paychecks. I'm so lucky that I have a supportive husband who enjoys his government job. He gives us security – if my income takes a nosedive, his income will keep us afloat while I pivot my business. Another way to help manage a self-publishing career is to keep your expenses as low as possible. Save money for leaner months. You don't have to be a millionaire to do this. The leaner your expenses, the more freedom you have to enjoy all the awesome stuff money can't buy. Amazing experiences, freedom, wonderful people, creative integrity... all the good stuff.

You get to live a truly unique life. You're an artist, so

people kind of expect you to be a bit strange. Lean into that, because why the hell not? You're fucking rock'n'roll.

You will butt heads with gatekeepers. You got two options – you can twist your work to fit what they want, or you can bypass them altogether. Both options have merit, and it comes down to what you want to achieve and what you need to survive. It's never a bad thing to take the payday that supports your family, as long as you stay true to your values.

What I see in my career is a big spike of income when I release a new book, then over time that spike will flatten out. But each time I release a book, the spike gets a little bigger and the flatline is a little bit more lucrative. If I'm a $200k a year author after 35 books, where will I be when I've published 50 books? 75? I can't wait to find out.

Being an author can be a bit of a rollercoaster. Sometimes a release won't do as well as you expect, or Amazon will glitch and, say, forget to send out your pre-order book, leading to hundreds of readers complaining and leaving bad reviews. Not that that's happened to me. Not at all. I love Amazon and my benevolent god Bezos...

The more frequently you release new content or conduct marketing efforts to grow your audience, the more you'll notice those spikes even out. Now, I'm at the point where I'm releasing something new (even if it's a shorter guide like this) practically every month. This helps my income to regulate across the year. I can better predict what I'm earning and plan for big launches and advertising.

Every book you write adds to your backlist – and that backlist will continue to earn you money for years to come. As I've said numerous times in this book, you set yourself up for success by keeping your backlist as tightly branded as possible, so more readers will binge *everything* you've got. In saying that, as you grow your reader base and your financial cushion, you can afford to take risks and try something different.

I love self-publishing because it's opened me up to the world of entrepreneurship. I feel as though I was born to be an entrepreneur. I love making something, putting it out into the world, and seeing what happens. If you're reading this book, I think you will, too.

And lastly, the best creative inspiration comes from a place of joy and acceptance. If you're not having fun, then ask yourself why that is. Are you excited about your writing? Is something else going on in your life you need to deal with? Are you still interested in being a writer? It's perfectly okay to take a step back, to change what you're doing, to slow down or speed up, to quit altogether.

You don't have to be miserable to be a great artist. Look after yourself. Deal with your shit. Be kind to others and the earth. Lift up your fellow artists, because this isn't a zero-sum game. Celebrate your successes and your failures. Have an absolute blast!

Write the book. Do the thing. Publish the book. Take over the world.

WHAT TO DO NEXT

The world of indie publishing is overwhelming. I get that. All you wanted to learn was how to publish a book, and I've just bombarded you with a whole ton of ideas and talk about your career and the future of reading.

In this section, we put everything we've just talked about together to create an action plan to get you from where you are right now to the next rung on the ladder of where you want to be. If you're reading this book because you want a clear path for success, then this is where you map it out.

In a very particular order, here's what I recommend you do.

DEFINE WHAT SUCCESS MEANS TO YOU

This is where you sit down and think about what you actually truly want from your writing. Brainstorm. Get creative. Don't be afraid to dream big – but remember, it has to feel authentic to you. It's all very well dreaming about fame and riches, but ask yourself why? Why do you want to be rich? If you don't do something with it, you just have a pile of money.

Boring. No one gets excited about that except maybe bankers and ducks.

Consider what you want to do with your life and the kind of person you strive to be. How do your books factor into that? Put some solid numbers on it – such as the amount of copies you want to sell. Consider the kind of stories you want to be known for – what's your author brand?

TAKE A CRITICAL LOOK AT YOUR ALREADY PUBLISHED WORK

If you've already dabbled with self-publishing, it's time to take an inventory. Look at:

- How many books you have.
- Are you letting your readers down in any areas?
- Do you need better editing, new covers, or an updated blurb?
- Do you have a cohesive author brand?

THINK ABOUT HOW YOU COULD CREATE A SERIES TO HOOK READERS

How do other authors in your genre tackle series? Can you expand your ideas or world to add series potential?

READ SOME SUCCESSFUL INDIE AUTHORS IN YOUR GENRE

Learn from their triumphs and mistakes. Look at their 'package' – the book itself, the cover, the blurb, the marketing. What's the experience they're giving readers? How can you deliver the same consistent experience?

DEFINE YOUR BRAND

Who are you as an author? What's the one sentence that describes your body of work? What do readers get when they pick up one of your books? Are there any elements of your brand that have been damaged? (For example, bad editing resulting in lots of low reviews for a book). It's time to get serious and take control of your brand.

START A MAILING LIST

Just do it already! If you do no other marketing for your books at all, you should do the mailing list.

MAKE DECISIONS

KU or wide? 6x9 or 5x8? Facebook or Instagram? Learning about self-publishing can feel so overwhelming. You can be paralyzed by the fear of getting it wrong.

When I feel like this, I give myself a short timeframe for a decision – "I have ten minutes" or "I have an hour." I read all the information I can find within that timeframe, then at the end, I make a decision. I don't waste any more time on it.

Sometimes that decision is right for me. Sometimes it's wrong. I only learn by doing. Very few decisions are black/white. It's better to get them out of the way and move forward than to wallow in indecisiveness.

DREAM BIG, AND HAVE FUN

For me, this is the most important thing. Being a successful indie author is hard – there are much easier ways to make money. So if you're not having fun, there's no point. You might as well be doing pretty much any other job. Sure, be strategic, think about the market, focus on your readers, but make sure you're enjoying yourself and you're proud of the stories you tell.

Now, go forth and write! I'll see you on the bestseller charts! And if you want to dig deeper into self-publishing and rocking your author career, consider joining me for *How to Rock Self-Publishing: The Course*.

GRAB MY FREE EBOOK

Make your passion for writing a driving force in your life.

You're embarking on an adventure full of intrigue and danger and flesh-eating dragons and hot, roadside tavern wenches who try to lure you off-course with their feminine wiles. My book, *Unleash the Beast: Releasing Your Inner Writing Monster*, will help you stay the course. You'll discover:

THAT BEHIND EVERY SUCCESSFUL CREATIVE IS A SOLID PROCESS.

With a process, you'll be able to work through anything life throws at you, including aforementioned flesh-eating dragons.

HOW TO EXPLORE AND NURTURE YOUR CREATIVE VOICE.

We'll explore the techniques I use alongside those of other successful authors to feed the inner creative beast

HOW YOU CAN ROCK A WRITING CAREER

How to go from being a hobby writer to getting paid work, selling books, and building a fun and successful writing business.

Get this ebook completely FREE:

https://www.
rageagainstthemanuscript.com/Unleashdownload

READY TO TAKE YOUR SELF-PUBLISHING TO THE NEXT LEVEL?

Join a group of passionate wordsmiths committed to success as you dig into *How to Rock Self-Publishing: The Course*.

Inspired by the popular self-publishing book by *USA Today* bestselling author Steff Green, this course gives you all the tools, advice, and encouragement you need to go from writing THE END to holding a copy of your book in your hands.

By using Steff's 11-step method for self-publishing success, you'll elbow your doubts in the face, stomp on the guesswork, and learn how to:

- Decide what, how, and when to publish.
- Get stuck into goal-setting and putting yourself on the path to success.
- Tame your monkey mind and consolidate your gazillion ideas into a solid plan.

- Choose the best platforms, editors, designers, and tools to create a high-quality book.
- Build a kickass author brand that keeps readers coming back for more.
- Plan a compelling book series in any genre that will have your readers chomping for more.
- Format and publish your work for ebook, print, and audiobook.
- Package your book to capture eyes and hearts, with brilliant cover design, blurbage, and a title that wows.
- Use metadata and other quick wins to help you book find its audience.
- Plan your future releases to set yourself up for success.
- Write faster, release more often, and enjoy what you create.
- Launch with a BANG! – including handy launch checklists and plans for different genres.
- Create an engaging author platform to turn your readers into lifelong fans.
- Spot trends and gaps in the market where you can add your unique voice.
- Find unique and emerging opportunities in self-publishing to build your audience and earn a living.
- Up-to-date industry news and the latest tips to help you ROCK.

Steff's 11-step method for self-publishing success broken down into easy-to-digest video and audio lessons, with worksheets, bonus content, resource lists, activities, and a community atmosphere where you can ask questions and share your successes and frustrations. Plus...

. . .

...**over ten hours of bonus audio content**, including interviews with top authors and publishing experts across a wide range of genres.

Your readers are waiting for you – are you ready to meet them?

Reserve your spot today: http:// rageagainstthemanuscript.com/howtorockcourse

(Suitable for beginner and intermediate authors, with an add-on author mastermind for those wanting to make writing their full-time career.)

Made in the USA
Columbia, SC
22 October 2021